I SEE OLD PEOPLE

A TRUE STORY ABOUT HOW SMALL ACTS
OF KINDNESS LEAD US TO EXTRAORDINARY LOVE
AND CONNECTIONS THAT DEFY OUR WILDEST DREAMS

JEANNE CORVESE HUSSIN

For Shirley, my mom, my biggest fan, my laughter, my heart and soul, my best friend. I wish you love.

Contents

Prologue

After spending fifteen wonderful years as a marketing executive for a large mortgage banking company, I was suddenly unemployed. It was the end of 2008, the financial crisis was beginning, the US housing bubble was bursting, and the values of securities tied to real estate were plummeting. I was a senior vice president for the largest independent mortgage banker in the country. Without warning, a larger financial institution swooped in to acquire my company.

During the acquisition, I had the choice of staying and taking a significant pay cut or receiving my contractual severance package. I didn't feel much like drinking the Kool-Aid, so I opted for the latter.

I had all sorts of ideas about how I would enjoy my generous yearlong severance package. I would take long hikes and travel with my then fourteen-year-old son, Jason. I would rearrange my furniture and pick out some new pieces for the patio. I thought about trying out speed dating too. After being legally separated for roughly two years, I felt ready to consider romance. I'd elected a legal separation because I had no intention of ever marrying again and knew Jason wasn't ready for another father. I was extremely independent, my life was full, I had lots of women friends, and I felt content.

Still, I enjoyed flirting with men. A LOT. I think in the back of my mind, I had a sliver of hope that Mr. Right would suddenly appear—on a grand scale. Something like *Sleepless in Seattle*.

So I did what thousands of women do—I went online. After Jason fell asleep at night, I began chatting with strangers. I was always careful to "underwrite" the candidate and meet in a public place. Despite my careful vetting, I still had my fair share of horror stories. Like the guy who asked me to meet him for a cocktail and after two drinks told me he'd need help paying the tab. What, you can't afford to buy me a drink? Ummmm, RED FLAG. No thank you.

Then there was the sales manager at the inn near where I worked. As we got to know each other online, he told me he knew our travel manager, Jill, who was a friend of mine. After a month of talking virtually, we agreed to meet. I quizzed Jill about this man and shared the photo of him—a drop-dead handsome guy who spent a lot of time at the gym.

"That's not Phil," Jill said, eyeing the photo.

"Are you sure it's not him?"

Jill emphatically stated, "There is *no* way this is Phil."

To my shock, she showed me a picture of the real Phil from the inn's website. This was *not* the guy in the dating site photo! Not in the slightest.

Sometimes I met men at the night spots I frequented, where I loved to dance (along with the flirting). I remember meeting one guy who asked me out only to cancel two weeks later, citing he'd met someone else. Really? You're closing the door to dating after just meeting someone new? Are you crazy? Oh, and it gets better … When things didn't work out with the other woman, he emailed me to see if I was interested in going out. ARE YOU KIDDING ME?

I had all this time on my hands, and online dating wasn't

working out, so speed dating seemed like a logical next step. My list of ideas was growing, yet I felt something was missing. Then it hit me. *Oh, I have time now. I can make a difference. Life has been good to me, so why not give back?*

Philanthropy was calling my name, or maybe God was nudging me. Whatever the case, I knew I had to do something and soon. It was early May by then, and I had been out of work for five months. I wouldn't be unemployed forever, and I could feel the time slipping by.

What possible excuse did I have with all this excess time? Clearly, I needed to concentrate on finding work. Yes, I could continue to rearrange the furniture. The dating thing was intoxicating. My son could be demanding. Surely a few hours a week wouldn't be out of the question.

Returning to work would only create more excuses. *I'm too tired. I don't have the time. Jason needs me. It isn't fair to make a commitment I can't keep.* If I didn't do something about this compulsion now, it wasn't going to happen.

After careful consideration, the only answer was, YES, I would do it. I'd felt increasingly drawn to spend time with seniors, so I looked on the internet for assisted living facilities in Simi Valley, California, where I lived. I was fairly certain there was a need for volunteers. How many people like to visit old age homes?

Wait a minute. Is this really what I want to do? These places smell. They're depressing. Death is lurking around every corner. Can I handle it?

Despite my best efforts to convince myself otherwise, I voted yes. I found a facility fifteen minutes from my house and called to inquire about volunteer opportunities. I was soon connected to Dora, the activities director.

"Hi, my name is Jeanne. I'm currently in between jobs and

wondered if you have any opportunities for me to volunteer with your residents?"

"Absolutely!" Dora said with an enthusiastic pitch. "I could sure use some help. We have two sides to our facility, and I have to work both. It's hard to do it all. There's our Recollections side, which houses our residents with Alzheimer's and dementia. Or you could help with our other residents who require less assistance."

I told her I was fine with the Recollections side. We agreed that I would come in for two hours that week.

Dora suggested things I could do with the residents like playing bingo, reading newspaper headlines, and asking engaging questions about their favorite places. Although I appreciated the suggestions, I knew I would just wing it. Conversation came naturally to me. I felt sure I had plenty to offer these new friends.

What I wasn't prepared for was what I would get in return.

Chapter 1

Caring for My Grandmother

In this life, we cannot do great things.
We can only do small things with great love.

—Mother Teresa

My mother, Shirley, was all about giving back. I think it was partly because she'd been on the receiving end of so many small acts of kindness, especially after my dad died. A widow at thirty-nine, she'd been a flamboyant and talented piano player with three small children to raise. After my father's death, offers of help came pouring in.

Dr. Frank Evan, a former musician buddy and good friend to my parents, provided us with free dental care. Other offers included free tickets to Orioles games for my two brothers, sleepovers at countless friends' homes, and as-needed house repairs from a well-intentioned neighbor who adored my father. The offers were endless and continued throughout my childhood.

The Bible teaches us that we reap what we sow. My mother was a testament to this teaching. She talked often about people "giving you the shirt off their back." At twelve years old, I wondered why anyone would want to do that, especially if they liked the shirt.

Later, I would understand well the meaning of giving away my shirt, my time, and my heart. It started with nursing my grandmother.

~

In 1977, I was sixteen years old, and my grandmother was dying of colon cancer. My mother and her two sisters, Bette and Delores, decided she would come to live in our home.

"She is going to die with dignity," my mother told Bette.

Bette remarked, "Of course, Shirley. We'll all take turns. I'll come every evening to relieve you, and Delores will come on the weekends."

Before the move, I visited my grandmother in the hospital, and I didn't like what I saw. She was weak, debilitated, and weaving in and out of consciousness. This was not the grand-mother I knew.

It was odd. She would talk to my mother as if she were a small child. She asked Aunt Bette if Shirley knew.

"Does Shirley know what?" asked Bette.

"That I'm dying," my grandmother said.

I wondered if my grandmother's short-term dementia was really an act of kindness from God. After all, she was visiting her youth. She was reliving the days of being a young mother, one of the most memorable periods of her life.

I was searching for a way to see death as a rebirth and not the dark and frightening place I feared it to be. I decided it was a blessing that my grandmother was somewhere else. In her condition, the present wasn't an attractive option.

When she came to our home, it was only a matter of weeks

before the end. My mother and her sisters traded shifts. My mom learned to give my grandmother rectal dilation to ease her pain.

Aunt Bette managed to find the humor in this unglamorous ritual. She imitated my mother putting on the latex gloves to prepare for "the treatment." The demonstration was brilliant, worthy of a *Saturday Night Live* award for best in show. My aunt methodically stretched the gloves up over her hands with the allure of a stripper removing her gloves for her audience. After donning the gloves, she turned ever so slowwwwwly so we would take notice of her "doctor" status. She pointed her index finger up and into the air, examining it closely, psyching herself up for this VERY important medical procedure.

After this theatrical imitation, my aunt and I would shriek with laughter. "Jeanne, leave it to your mother to make a rectal dilation into an academy award performance!"

The laughter was good. It was a welcome release amid the stress and sadness that my mom and aunts were experiencing as my grandmother neared the end of her life.

One day I was alone with my grandmother, helping her with the lunchtime meal.

"Do you mind?" she asked.

"Mind what?" I said.

"Mind having to feed me."

I lowered the spoon and paused to consider. My throat tightened. I held back the tears because I didn't want my grandmother to see me cry. I wanted to wail. After all she'd been through, she wondered if it was hard on me. *Oh my God, no.*

"I don't mind at all," I said and continued with the feeding.

Chapter 2

Put Your Teeth In, Please

My mother was quite the character. In fact, I would say the entire neighborhood where I grew up in Baltimore would tell you the same about her.

After my father died, my mother began drinking. Back then, "pills" were considered objectionable while alcohol was perfectly okay. In fact, in the 1970s, the police would actually stop you if you were drinking and offer you a ride home. It seems crazy by today's standards.

In hindsight, I would characterize my mom as a functioning alcoholic. My two brothers and I lived in a middle class home, were well cared for, and were fed three meals a day. I lived what I considered a normal life. Years later, in her fifties, my mom quit drinking cold turkey, having confessed to me that she would drink up to ten beers a day. If I tried that with my small frame, I would need to be rushed to the nearest ER.

Despite her addiction, she was able to work an occasional music job, take care of three small children, feed our dogs, and take care of our home. My grandmother and my mom's sisters were all strong and dominant and played key roles in our growing up years.

My mom could often be found smoking a cigarette and

enjoying a beer while peering out the kitchen window, waiting for something to light up her busybody radar. She always had a streak of childlike mischief.

My aunt Bette, who lived with us when she was in between jobs, had a very loud, obnoxious laugh. It rolled off her tongue and sounded like a jackhammer, *EEH, EEH, EEH.*

My mother would chime along, *AHH, AHH, AHH,* grabbing me by the arm and shaking me violently until I was forced to laugh along with her.

They were one-of-a-kind characters, and at sixteen years of age, I was rightfully embarrassed by them.

My aunt had a full set of dentures, and my mom a partial denture bridge. Both had their teeth out more often than not and housed them in Tupperware bowls by the kitchen window—within reach should someone stop by the house.

One beautiful summer evening, I was expecting my date to arrive any minute. Seeing my mother and Aunt Bette sitting around with their cigarettes and Pabst Blue Ribbon beer, laughing wildly, I panicked and pleaded with them to put their dentures in before my date drove up.

"Please, PLEEEEEASE, put your teeth in," I gasped. "My date will be here any minute. I'm begging you!"

My aunt turned her head to me and grinned wickedly, revealing her gums. She thundered, "Relax, we have plenty of time!" My mother chimed in with her boisterous laugh. They were a duet of laughing hyenas delighting at my look of dismay.

It's too late!

My date's car was already pulling into the driveway.

"Hurry up!" I screamed. "He's in the driveway NOW. For the love of God, put your teeth in."

It's over. Once he sees THEM, he's never coming back.

Then, it happened. My aunt rushed to the sink to put in her dentures. When she turned around, a strand of our spiderwort plant was lodged in her teeth and dangling down the side of her mouth!

"Will you look at me?" she erupted with unstoppable giggles. "This plant got stuck to my teeth!" *EEH, EEH, EEH.*

Oh my God, someone adopt me. Someone take me away from this insanity. I will never get married. Never, ever. Who will have me with these two around?

It got worse. When my date knocked on the door, my mom answered. "Why, hello! Come on in, Jack," she pronounced with the affected tones of an actress ready to tell her first joke.

Shaking Jack's hand, she looked at me and said, "Now, Jeanne, I don't think his arms are too short for his body." *AHH, AHH, AHH.*

I was lucky this time. My date managed a laugh, and I hurried to grab his arm and rush him out the door before anything else could be said to threaten my love life.

Today I'd give anything to see my mom and Aunt Bette—with or without their dentures. I feel fortunate to have inherited their gift of humor. I can still hear their laughter. It's alive deep inside of me, and I keep it close at hand when I need a good chuckle. Teeth or no teeth.

Chapter 3

The Framework for Empathy

I was nine years old when I watched my father die. He asked me to have my mother call the ambulance. He grabbed my hand and told me he loved me.

After calling the paramedics and returning to the bedroom, my mother begged him to hold on. Though he was in excruciating pain, he fought to stay alive. His anger flared and he cursed the Lord for deciding it was his time to go. He put his fist through the wall, exclaiming, "Jesus, Mary, and Joseph." I don't think he was saying it in the biblical sense. After all, he was only forty-three.

My brothers and I were quickly handed over to neighbors while my mother accompanied my father in the ambulance. She would later tell the story of someone hitting my father in the chest to jumpstart his heart while he was being lifted into the ambulance. I'm not sure if she or a paramedic administered the blow.

Before he died, he'd suffered three other heart attacks, the first at age thirty-nine. He had arteriosclerosis and a severely damaged heart. After he died, the doctor told my mom he had the arteries of a seventy-three-year-old man. That July, he'd started having symptoms that prompted the doctor to recommend bed rest. Looking back, that seems absurd for someone who'd suffered three major heart attacks.

There wasn't much to be done, and he died within an hour of arriving at the local hospital. I recall the doctor telling my mother they tried everything, including inserting a pacemaker. He apologized and explained that if he'd known her husband was going to pass in this way, he would have hospitalized him earlier.

Experiencing death at such a young age leaves an indelible mark. I prayed that night that God would save my dad. I assumed this was just another one of his heart attacks and that he would recover as he had in the past. With the medicine we had at the time and pacemaker technology, surely he would make it.

After he died, I reflected on my daydreams over the previous year. *What would it be like if Dad died? I'd get so much attention, and people would do anything to please me. I would be popular.*

I was the kind of kid picked last to be on the school sports team. So, as I envisioned a circle of friends hovering around me, consoling me, and making me feel like I fit in, it felt like a perfect world.

Wait a minute. I don't really want my dad to die. It's wrong to feel this way. This isn't right. I feel bad even thinking these thoughts. My journey with guilt was just beginning.

How does a nine-year-old make sense of such a confusing and painful loss? *My thoughts must have triggered his death. God didn't answer my prayers because I had bad thoughts.* I was certain I'd caused this terrible event. I never told my mother. I kept it inside. Any strange thoughts became a continual source of guilt for me.

In my adult years, I wondered if this triggered minor OCD (obsessive-compulsive disorder). I began having strange out-of-the box thoughts that troubled me. Because I'd thought about my dad dying before he actually died, subconsciously I felt responsible. So I began compulsively questioning every thought that came into my head. Looking back, I think it was a form of self-punishment. Whenever my mom left my brothers and me alone at night, I checked the door locks and the stove knobs multiple times. I was stressed and afraid she would die too; I needed to make sure everything was safe.

Then I learned compassion. My mother taught me about the etiquette of death. I overheard her phone conversations on the subject.

"Bette, I'm so damn tired of people telling me they understand when they've never lost a husband. The other day Jill had the audacity to compare her divorce grief with my pain. She said, 'Well, at least Dick didn't leave you like my husband did.' How dare she do that? She's not helping me. She has no right to make that comparison. There's NO comparison to what I went through with losing Dick!" My mom sobbed over the phone.

Over the years, my mom had nightmares about my dad rejecting her instead of dying. Subconsciously and irrationally, I think she felt he left her on purpose.

"I've even had people tell me I'll meet someone new. I don't want to meet someone else. There will never be another someone!" I overheard her say. True to her word, there wasn't.

Without knowing, my mother taught me how to help people in grief.

"Never say you understand, Jeanne, unless you really do," my mother said.

"Why, Mom?"

"Well, if you haven't lost your husband, you don't

understand what it feels like. For example, I would never tell someone who lost a child that I understand. I don't because, thank God, I haven't experienced it," she explained.

"What should people say, Mom?"

She paused before answering, "Nothing. Absolutely nothing. Just listen."

~

It was her turn now. My mom was two months shy of turning sixty-six. After her years of heavy drinking and smoking, she developed squamous cell carcinoma, better known as cancer of the throat. Her doctor told me that, according to some studies, the risk of these cancers in heavy drinkers and smokers may be as much as 100 times more than in those who don't imbibe. Statistically, nearly seventy percent of patients with oral cancer are heavy drinkers.[1]

My mother was hospitalized sometime in February of 1997, when the malignant tumor had grown on her tongue and into her throat. I was mortified when the doctor said to me, "She may lose her tongue."

My family and I were so relieved when the doctor saved her tongue and successfully removed the malignancy. While my mother initially survived the first surgery, she had to remain connected to a tracheal tube, which meant she couldn't speak. It became difficult to interpret what she needed as she could only communicate by writing.

Her body and her hands were significantly weakened by the disfiguring surgical procedure. At times, I felt I was trying

---

1 "Risk Factors for Oral Cavity and Oropharyngeal Cancers," American Cancer Society, Revised March 9, 2018, https://www.cancer.org/cancer/oral-cavity-and-oropharyngeal-cancer/causes-risks-prevention/risk-factors.html.

to decipher a child's scribbles.

Watching her die was excruciatingly painful. It was my first adult experience with the health care system. Everything I learned about compassion from my mother was put to the test. She had some great health care providers ... and then there were those I went to battle with, sobbing for mercy on my mother's behalf.

One day, my mother wrote frantically, requesting an enema. When I asked the nurse to help me with my mom's request, the nurse shot me an annoyed look and told me to wait. In her opinion, this wasn't a critical situation.

Yes, it is, I thought. My mother was trapped in her body and unable to communicate. She struggled with irritable bowel syndrome most of her later years, and I knew if she felt uncomfortable, she needed that enema. I wasn't going to let her suffer.

In the movie *Terms of Endearment*, Shirley MacLaine's character pleads with the on-call nurse to relieve her daughter's pain. She screams like a madwoman: "GIVE HER THE SHOT... GIVE MY DAUGHTER THE SHOT!" I felt like her, only I was shouting, "GIVE HER AN ENEMA! GIVE MY MOTHER AN ENEMA!"

I ran to the closest doctor to escalate the procedure. *"Please,"* I begged, "my mother really needs to have an enema. She's really upset. Please help me." The doctor was compassionate and moved quickly to get someone to help my mother.

The nurse was pissed. "Why did you go around me?"

"Can't you see? My mom is crying out for help. She's my mother. She can't talk. She's totally helpless. Please, I beg you to understand. What if it were your mom? Wouldn't you do the same thing?"

Meanwhile, my mother kept looking at me as if to say, "What in the hell are they waiting for?"

Please hurry up, she scribbled on the writing pad. Then she accused me of acting like Mrs. Wiggins, a secretarial character played by Carol Burnette in the seventies, who moved with the slowness of molasses. Even as she was dying, my mother had humor.

When someone finally came to give my mother the enema, I was relieved yet so overwhelmed by the whole situation that I needed to step out for some air. I began to convulse with heaving sobs. I was disgusted at myself for being so weak.

My mother never pleaded. She didn't beg. She told people what she wanted and what she thought. I had to cry like a baby. It hurt so bad. I didn't understand people without compassion. I vowed that one day I would make people understand.

They weren't all that way, though some had to be guided toward compassion. Another nurse got cross with me when I asked her to help me find a piece of swab cloth to tend to my mother's drooling. "Look," she said, "I have patients with many more serious complications. You will have to wait."

Sheepishly, I turned to my mute mother. Her face asked, "What did she just say to you?"

"Mom, don't worry about it. I don't want to say anything to her that would compromise your care."

The nurse overheard what I said. *Uh-oh. She's coming over to me.*

She reprimanded me in front of my mother. "I would never do that," she said. "I will take care of your mother. Just give me time."

I was furious. Protective even to the end, my mother sensed when her baby cub wasn't being treated properly. I marched outside of her intensive care cubicle and addressed the nurse with gut-wrenching emotion.

"Look, I may lose my mom. I don't know what's going to happen. I'm afraid and I have never been through this before. I was trying to help you out by doing the procedure myself. Then you come in and reprimand me in front of my mother. I don't want her to be upset. I don't know how much time I have with her! Can't you understand?"

I broke down into choking sobs. The nurse slowly and compassionately put her arms around me. "I'm sorry," she said. I forgave her.

Admittedly, it was much harder to forgive the "enema" nurse. I decided to take a different perspective. This wasn't about me. This was a teachable moment. My mother's biggest life lesson for me was about "listening and understanding." I chose to believe that I taught the nurses empathy. Somehow, my words would resonate with them. As a result, they would act differently, with kindness and respect toward the next patient in the room.

~

I posted a gorgeous photo of my mother in her late twenties on her hospital room bulletin board. It was an aha moment for me. *If the staff sees the mother I see, the person she really is, they'll treat her with kindness. If they know Shirley's story and Shirley's gift, they'll understand. AHA.*

The woman in the photo was a buxom blonde, a professional piano player and singer whose frosty voice earned her comparisons to Sarah Vaughan. She had luminous ivory skin, and she carried herself with confidence. My father once wrote in a love letter to my mother, "When you walk into the room, the whole room lights up."

She was feminine, strong, funny, and feisty. She used to say, "Jeanne, I tell it like it is." That could be disastrous for anyone sitting on her bad side. If she liked you, you were one lucky person. If she didn't, you knew it and cowered beneath her piercing gaze. My friend once said, "Your mom scares me." She scared me too. Yet, I knew she adored me and I was her everything. I was her friend and confidante, her pride and joy.

The photo of her would tell her story. It was a black-and-white professional glamour photo from the 1950s. Wearing a halter dress and gold roped earrings, she faced the camera head on. Her lips were full and painted with a rich, dark lipstick. She smiled with a toothy overbite, and her large beautiful brown eyes twinkled. She looked a little naughty, yet warm and sweet … someone you'd want to be friends with and tell all your stories to—especially the juicy ones.

When I posted the photo, I immediately felt a sense of relief. *There, now things will be different. Now you can speak, Mom. People will really know who you are. They will like you and want to be your friend.*

I looked over at my mom. Her eyes were half shut. She was breathing with the help of machines and tubes. She was disfigured and wasting away. As for me, I could see she was still there in a physical body that was deteriorating minute by minute.

"Isn't she beautiful?" I said to one of the rotating male nurses, pointing out my mother's photo.

"Wow, she sure is," he said with an approving nod. "She looks like Marilyn Monroe."

"I know. People told her that a lot. She was incredible. She was a fabulous entertainer and worked in Las Vegas with my dad, who was a talented saxophone player. She played piano and he played sax. It was the perfect match. They worked in Vegas in the fifties when it was really something. My mom was always entertaining and making people laugh."

"Gosh, that's amazing. I bet you were so proud of her," he said, flashing me a smile.

"I was. I mean, I am," I said. "I wish you could have known her like I do."

The photo seemed to be the magic bullet I needed. Every time someone saw it, it told Shirley's story. It invited commentary, thoughtfulness, and most importantly compassion. It spoke a thousand words. And it allowed me to speak about the REAL Shirley, not the one hooked up to the machines.

How ironic it was for me years later when I saw young photos of my Recollections residents plastered outside each one's room. The intention was the same. I thought to myself, here are all beautiful people with a rich history, a story to tell, a meaning by which they lived their lives.

There was the beloved school teacher, the medaled World War II hero, the engineer, and the laboratory technician who wanted to be a doctor—each one carrying a beaming smile of joy.

The first time I saw them, I remembered posting my mother's photo in her hospital room and the many conversations it sparked. I wanted to know the stories behind the weathered faces. I wanted to understand how they touched people. I wanted to know them beyond their physical limitations. And with a few miracles, I would.

The Meeting

I have no idea what I'm going to say or do as I arrive at Recollections. Yet I know I'm good at thinking on my feet. Plus, I'm a natural at talking to strangers.

Okay, so this might be a little more one-sided than talking to strangers. After all, this is the "difficult side."

After exchanging pleasantries, Dora leads me to the other side of the facility. We approach a double-door entrance requiring a security code to get in and out.

Wow, the residents are on lockdown.

Far from the austere prison vibe I've been imagining, though, the hallways are painted with beautiful depictions of a different era, full of hope and optimism. Music from the 1930s and 40s plays through the halls. I recognize the brilliant lyrics and haunting tune of "I'll Be Seeing You," a hugely popular WWII-era song addressing the pain of separation, particularly for soldiers who went off to war.

I spot memory boxes filled with photos, a mannequin draped in a cream-colored bridal dress, hats of various eras hanging off a rack, and several Norman Rockwell prints adorning the walls. At first, it doesn't smell as bad as I expected. I'm pleased to catch the aroma of freshly baked cookies as we approach the kitchen. This place feels homey.

Entering the formal gathering room, I spot the residents scattered about. A few are slumped down in their wheelchairs, staring into space. Others are seated in pairs on sofas, and a few loners are circled around the wide-screen television set. I introduce myself with an over-the-top, loud, and enthusiastic greeting. "Well, HELLLOOOO, everyone."

A few curious glances turn my way. One woman is protesting, furiously kicking her legs at two aides trying to calm her down. Dora moves toward them and tries to defuse the situation by addressing the woman directly. "Sara Beth, what's wrong? You can't kick the aides, darling. You could hurt them."

She turns to give me a bemused look. When she returns to stand beside me, she whispers, "She's never like this. I've never seen her act like this before."

An aide asks Dora if I'm a family member.

"No. This is Jeanne. She's a volunteer. Welcome, Jeanne."

I look at Dora and whisper, "It's okay," signaling that she can leave me alone with the residents.

"If it gets too tough, you can always work the other side," she assures me before sauntering out of the room.

The aides are still here, of course, and they seem happy to have a fresh face in the room. It's really hot in here, especially for a woman in perimenopause and expecting many more hot flashes on the horizon. There's a faint smell of urine and an even stronger smell of feces. How do the aides stand to be around it for eight hours a day? They must be saints … or perhaps they just get used to it and move on.

I choose a seat in the middle of the room and start my visit. Despite the sweltering heat and the occasional pandemonium, I'm going to be cheerful. I'm going to make a difference. I'm going to give them an hour or so of sunshine.

"Helloooooooooooo, everyone. My name is Jeanne and I'm a volunteer. Howwwww are you all today? Well, I thought I would just have a friendly chat with you. You see, I lost my job at a large mortgage company, and it seems I have some time on my hands. I can't seem to attract a man, so I really don't have much of a life. So here I am!"

Bursts of laughter echo around the room. *Amazing!* They get it. They get me. They understand my humor. I have an audience, and they like me. This feels good.

I continue my one-sided dialogue, determined to keep them laughing.

"It's really hot in here. That's dangerous for a woman in menopause."

More laughter.

"Anyway, I just got back from a vacation to Boston where I reunited with my Italian relatives. My son and I had a fabulous time. Did any of you travel? What cities did you like best?"

A woman who introduces herself as Nancy chimes in, "We had an RV and traveled everywhere. It was wonderful." She's a lovely woman with a contagious smile. There's an indescribable warmth about her. Unlike some of the other residents who start to nod off, she giggles at almost everything I say.

"You did? Tell me about your RV. What was it like and where did you go?"

"Well, it was very large. It had everything in it. I cooked in it. I had Girl Scout meetings in it. It was wonderful."

"Where did you go?"

Nancy hesitates. She looks up as if she might find the answer in the air. Then her face clouds in confusion.

Oh, now I get it. She doesn't remember.

"Um, I don't really know," she replies.

"That's okay. It sounds like you had a great time wherever you went."

As Nancy and I get to know each other, I piece together that she worked as some sort of office manager. She tells me she was good in math and did "all sorts of things" in her job. She was a Girl Scout troop leader, she loved to sew, and she had three daughters.

"Nancy, you've got to make me a dress. In fact, I'm putting you all to work in this room! Nancy can sew a dress for me, Denise can help me get a man, and Jamie can cook for me. How about it, ladies?"

The room erupts in laughter.

"Nancy, if you were going to make me a dress, what color would it be?"

She giggles and cheers, "Red!"

"Why, that's my color, Nancy. I can't believe I'm that transparent!"

When it's time to leave, I feel light as air. My heart is full and I can't wait to come back.

The weeks fly by and I relish my time at Recollections. In no time at all, the residents become my friends. Some days are better than others. Sometimes, I give them all my energy and they suck the life out of me.

One day, a resident yells, "Help me. Help me. Get me out of here." There's nothing I can do. I just stop talking and wait for her to stop screaming.

Joan, one of my favorite residents, tells her to shut the hell up.

Oh, this is going to be fun.

Once she does finally settle down, I can't seem to get back on course with my conversation.

"PLEASE. Someone help me." There she goes again. It's the tenth time she's asked for help, and her vocal cords are starting to sound strained. How frightening it must be to have to shout for help. Is this some sort of drug-induced psychosis or simply dementia at its worst? I say a silent prayer, try to ignore it, and move on.

"Mary, where do you want to go?" quips one of the aides. I notice how often the aides rely on humor to manage the temporary insanity.

"Mary, you can't go outside. You have to stay here, honey."

Joan gets feisty again. "I'll tell her where to go. She can go outside and roll under a car, dammit!"

Joan is arguably one of the more intelligible women at Recollections. When we first met, she was talkative, understandable, and VERY direct. She and I hit it off right away. Heavier set with a head of short unruly curls, she has an edge to her and talks out of the side of her mouth with a slight lisp. She has no patience for outbursts and takes every single one of them personally.

She doesn't hold back when she feels strongly about something; my mom was like that. Joan "tells it like she sees it," as the expression goes. As long as her negative comments aren't directed toward me, I'm fine with it.

It's not uncommon for the residents to get unsettled and even angry at one another. After a few sharp comebacks, their spats are usually over. They are so childlike. It's as if they are back in kindergarten with no clear understanding of cause and effect. It's bittersweet. While their innocence and honesty are refreshing, their fear and confusion are like a nightmare. I can't help hoping I don't end up like this.

Chapter 4

Coping with Grief and Separation

My mom struggled through two more surgeries to try to repair some adhesions and then it was time to let her go. She died in the hospital on March 17, 1997, just shy of her sixty-sixth birthday.

The day of her death, my younger brother and I said our goodbyes and left the hospital sometime in the late morning. Once the doctors stopped some of her medications, her death was inevitable. I couldn't bear to have her taken off her ventilator. I worried she'd gasp for breath, and the thought pushed me over the edge.

My brother thought it was better for us to go. He said, "Mom wouldn't want us to watch her die." I remember thinking he was probably right. I threw myself into his arms and wailed like an injured wild animal struggling to stay alive. I couldn't breathe. I couldn't believe it was time. I didn't want to let her go.

My grief lasted for more than a year. It was the kind of grief that puts a knot in your throat every time you think of the person you lost. My son was my saving grace. The joys and demands of raising a spirited toddler forced me to move forward.

As a mother, I felt my mom with me throughout the journey. Jason was definitely a demanding, high-energy child. I made a lot of mistakes and was hard on myself. When I got upset about how I'd handled something, I would hear her gentle words, "It's okay. You're learning. He's going to be a great kid. And you're a wonderful mother."

What didn't work out was my marriage. The pressures of raising a defiant child led to many disagreements. So by the time I hit forty-five, I was a single mom with an eleven-year-old son. I became the primary parent when Jason's father moved a few hours away from our home. It was hard on Jason, and he blamed me for pretty much everything.

I felt very alone, especially at night after Jason went to bed and I was exhausted from the workday. I couldn't do anything right. Looking back, I was in a rush to do everything. Get him to school. Get to work on time. Pick him up from the aftercare program that he despised. Eat healthy—eat quickly. Help him with homework. Arguments. GUILT. GUILT. GUILT.

Looking back, I wish I could tell my younger self to relax more and worry less. I would say, "You're a great mother. It's not about whether he eats Kentucky Fried Chicken for the third week in a row. It's about how you show love, how you model kindness, how you focus on the things that really matter." I'd tell myself to slow down and enjoy the joyful moments more and think less about the painful moments. Aha. If only we had a crystal ball.

And then there was dating. I guess I needed an endorphin pick-me-up. And Match.com had just the thing. After putting Jason to bed for the evening, I'd jump on the computer and enjoy the many winks my profile had earned. I didn't realize how addicting and intoxicating it would become. Unfortunately, it was highly one-dimensional.

When Jason was about fourteen, I met one man online that I thought could be "the one." John was handsome, shared my liberal views, and had one son close in age to mine. He spoke kind words about his ex-wife, and he was a great kisser.

During that period, I never introduced Jason to anyone I met. I was careful to keep my dating life separate from my family life because my son was still very attached to his dad, and I knew that he wasn't emotionally ready for a steady influx of men in my life. I met men on my time, and that meant when I could grab a sitter or when Jason was spending a weekend with his father.

John and I dated for about three months. It ended sometime around Christmas when I became a little too aggressive about wanting more from him. At the time, I was devastated, even though I was not at all in love with him.

I saw this as further evidence that most men were selfish and burdensome. I carried that thinking for quite some time. It would take a while for me to change my tape. When I finally did, WOW, it was game over.

The Socialite

G ail is another favorite resident of mine. She appears to have command of her faculties. Even Dora wonders why she's on the Recollections side.

Gail is a perky, vivacious woman. The first time I met her, her lively blue eyes and beautifully coifed short hairdo made an immediate impression. Always well dressed with manicured nails and nicely matching jewelry, she is clearly a woman of means.

She tells me she lived in Burbank right up the street from Debbie Reynolds. When I mention Elizabeth Taylor and talk about the Eddie Fisher affair, Gail can't remember the incident. *This has to be dementia.* Anyone of her era knew about Eddie Fisher and Elizabeth Taylor.

Gail has two children, a loving husband, and a snappy comeback always on standby. When I reveal my dating mishaps, she replies, "Why, just stop doing that. If you aren't getting results, do something different." Or my favorite reply, "Why, once they set their eyes on you, they run the other direction!" which she snorts playfully.

I love it. I love her.

She is the light of the room. Gail listens intently to my stories and is always happy to share a few of her own. She likes to tell the story about the stranger that ended up in her swimming pool. She has repeated the story to me at least half a dozen times. I laugh every time as if it were the first time. Why not?

"Here I was sitting at my sewing machine when I see this woman saunter by with a bathing cap on. The next thing I know, I hear my back gate swing open and SPLASH, someone's in my pool," Gail says, her eyes wide as saucers.

"Well, I walk to the backyard and see this woman with the bathing cap on swimming in my pool! It's the woman up the street. Her son played with my son. I said, 'What in the hell do you think you are doing?'

"'Why, I'm taking a dip in your pool. Your son said it would be okay,' said the neighbor."

I can't believe anyone in their right mind would dare do such a thing without asking the adult first! What a crazy story—and funny too.

"I said to the lady, 'Well, it's not okay. Anyone that's gonna swim in my pool has to have my permission and I have to be here! What if something was to happen and I wasn't around? I'm responsible for my property. Now you get the hell out of my pool immediately,'" she recounts with a saucy tone.

Gail is not afraid. She is bold and forthcoming. You always know what's on her mind. My mother would have liked her.

Over time, I start putting pieces together. Gail is the lady with the social network. She claims she worked for my former CEO, who was almost a celebrity until the mortgage business went under. Gail is a scout leader, a swimmer, a seamstress, a cook, and a traveler. She owns an RV too and has traveled to many places. Most of them, she can't remember. She remembers Vegas, though. When I'm old, I hope I remember Vegas.

Gail is extremely quick-witted. Not the type who is sarcastic and mean spirited, Gail has the kind of wit that gives you a hearty belly laugh.

One day I ask the residents at what age they married.

"I was eighteen. Back then, that's what you did," says one resident.

"I didn't get married until I was thirty," says another.

"Wow. You waited quite a long time before getting tied down," I respond.

Gail quips, "Tied down? Honey, you haven't lived until you've been tied down!"

I almost fall off my chair. What a brilliant delivery! Gail's timing is impeccable. The entire room breaks into hysterics. They all get the humor, as do I.

Chapter 5

Wanting to Be Lady Diana

At some point in my life, I decided I wanted to be Lady Diana. I was essentially the same person. Okay, I wasn't shy, incredibly beautiful, or soft spoken. The one thing I did have in common with her was her gift of love.

Lady Diana once said, "I think the biggest disease the world suffers from in this day and age is the disease of people feeling unloved. I know that I can give love for a minute, for half an hour, for a day, for a month, but I can give. I am very happy to do that, I want to do that."[2]

Over the years, I watched Diana in the media. Like many others, I was inexplicably drawn to her beauty, her delicate voice, and her passion for people. She truly was "the people's princess."

I could relate to her acts of kindness. Plain and simple, she comforted people. She would walk into a room, grab the hand of an AIDS patient, and look into their eyes. For that moment in time, the patient felt extraordinary.

While Jason was growing up, I would often think about my next chapter in life. I could see myself being the person who

---

2   "Princess Diana Quotes," BrainyQuote, accessed February 3, 2021, https://www.brainyquote.com/quotes/princess_diana_127197.

gives back. Yet, I didn't have the time or energy to do much since I was a single working mom shouldering most of the parental responsibility.

I remember thinking, *I want to comfort people like Diana does. I can do that. I'm good with people. They trust me. They open up to me. I should do something like that.*

Then came the excuses and rationalizations. *Of course Lady Di can do that, she has millions of dollars and oodles of time. If I had the time and money, it would be easy for me too.*

I concluded I just had too many responsibilities. How could I possibly fit any sort of volunteerism into my life? It just wouldn't be fair. After all, with my business travel, I was already gone enough and missed more than I wanted of my son's development.

While it would have to wait, I wasn't giving up on the idea. I remember writing in a journal: *My goal is to make a difference in the world.* In my mind, I was making money to buy myself the freedom to one day do what I really wanted to do in life, to make a difference in people's lives.

Somehow, I knew it would involve older people. I felt it was my niche, my calling, my personal gift. I remembered the days I'd spent with my grandmother while she lived with us near the end. It was easy for me to talk to seniors, to hold their hands, to make them laugh.

My mother once told me, "Jeanne, you don't have a mean bone in your body." She saw in me a sweetness, a gentleness. I knew I had a "magical power" to make people feel good. And when I made someone feel good, the stage lights went up and it was show time! I was the star in my own little world, and I loved giving people the opportunity to smile and laugh.

I put that talent on the back burner for many years.

However, my mind didn't forget. There was something more I needed to do. I knew it and my subconscious knew it too.

Through the years, I found occasional opportunities to perform charitable acts. There was no better feeling in the world. I went to a few senior homes and delivered holiday gifts. I gave blood and donated money to all sorts of causes—the Red Cross, the Disaster Relief Fund, and the Cancer Society, to name a few. I adopted families for Christmas and took great care in hand-selecting the perfect gift for each child in the family.

Once when Jason was about twelve years old, I adopted a needy family for Christmas. I called my local charity and they suggested I provide gifts for a single father with two children.

When I called the father to find out what the children needed, he was humbled by my willingness to help and invited me to deliver the gifts at their home. I liked the idea, and I felt it would be a good experience for Jason.

The father explained his wife had left him and moved out of state. He was having problems finding work, and his six-year-old son was a real handful—a good boy, and at the same time, a real handful. I chuckled and said, "I have a real handful myself. I know full well the demands of raising a spirited and willful boy!"

His twelve-year-old daughter, on the other hand, was the "little mother." Forced into the unfortunate position of being the caregiver in the family, she was the proverbial good daughter, the mender, the fixer, the daddy champion—the one who could make things better.

What a burden, I thought as he went on to tell me he didn't know what he would do without her. The conversation broke my heart. I told him I would most definitely take care of his little girl for Christmas. I knew just what to get her.

When we arrived at the home, my son wanted to race to the door first. He knew we had a bundle of stuff to hand out, and he couldn't wait to see the expression on the family's faces. I bought seven or eight items for each child, including expensive electronic toys for the little boy. For the remarkable young lady, I purchased lots of pink girly girl stuff and trendy clothing I thought would delight the sensibilities of a preteen.

For the down-on-his luck father, I made a beautiful gift basket full of food, canned goods, and homemade cookies. I included a $75 gift card from the local grocer and a nice bottle of wine. He would need the wine to get through the holidays, I thought.

When we got to the front door, the little boy squealed in delight. He raced around in circles and chanted, "I want to open it. I want to open it." His father tried to get his son to contain his enthusiasm. I told the man it was quite alright and the little boy could open the packages right away.

The little boy wasted no time ripping open the packages and tossing the paper across the floor. He was ecstatic when he unwrapped the PlayStation game. He put it into the console and sat down to play it right away.

The father was thrilled. He told me I was right on the money and the gifts were generous beyond his wildest imagination. He looked at my son and said, "I hope you realize what a wonderful mom you have."

I beamed with pride. I hoped this day would stay in my son's memory bank and that one day he would adopt a family of his own at Christmas.

Before long, Jason jumped in to help the small boy with his

video game. When Jason failed to make the appropriate game move, the young boy stomped his feet, enraged. Finding his reaction rather humorous, we all began to chuckle. Well, this sent the young man into overdrive.

He yelled, "I'm going to shoot you," and then disappeared up the stairs.

We weren't laughing anymore, and the humiliated father tried to take control of the situation, bringing his son down-stairs and gently reprimanding the boy. "Now don't do this. You know this isn't right. Let's settle down now. You'll have a time out if you don't behave."

The sister rolled her eyes and said, "Now you see what I have to live with." She looked at me with a combination of embarrassment and exasperation.

Just then, the boy grabbed the household fire extinguisher and threatened to shoot all of us. I was bemused, shocked, and a little worried that this tantrum was going to spiral out of control. As one wise person once said, "No good deed goes unpunished."

I managed to let the child know we were very sorry and gently tried to encourage him to come down to earth. Everyone in the room was uncomfortable, and I knew the man would be glad when the whole episode was behind us.

My heart ached for this father who was trying at all costs to avoid an even bigger scene. Having dealt with Jason's emotional tantrums, I wanted to do everything I could to make this man feel that it was okay, that I understood.

When we left, my son walked away having learned several lessons. Number one: tantrums are really bad from the outside looking in. Number two: giving is good.

"Mom, was I ever like that?" Jason asked as we walked to the car.

"Well, not exactly, although you've had similar moments. Most importantly, the dad has a lot on his plate and you can see it was wonderful to be able to provide his children with a special Christmas. Don't you agree?"

"Yeah, Mom. Now can we go to Walmart and look for that PlayStation game for me for Christmas?" he asked.

Yes, no good deed goes unpunished.

Meeting John

John is the only man in the room among many women. "John, what a lucky guy you are. All these ladies and you're the only man in town!"

He grins from ear to ear and radiates an inner warmth. John is a big man with some girth on him, quite possibly from a few years of inactivity, and he always wears a baseball cap. He usually nods off after I start talking. When he's alert, though, his smiles and twinkling eyes melt your heart.

He can't remember much of anything. When I ask him if he had children, he pauses to consider and grimaces. "I don't know." I can tell it frustrates him. Unlike some of the other residents, he can't provide details to any questions about his life, his career, or his family.

I start to fill in the blanks. I figure he was the all-around nice guy with a big family and a solid career. He took care of his family and didn't have a temper. He liked to fish and loved sports and was a man's man as well as a woman's man. Yep, that was John alright. With a ready smile and a gentle nature, he was the kind of man any woman would be lucky to have. Turns out, my assumptions are right on the money.

During this week's visit, John sits in on an elementary card game I'm leading for a few of the residents. He's having trouble identifying his cards. Meanwhile, a very attractive blonde enters the room. I surmise she's either someone's relative or a health care provider, so I continue on with the game.

"John, do you have a queen?"

John squints and studies his cards with the intensity of a surgeon preparing to operate. I can see he's holding a queen. I wait patiently to see if John will find it on his own.

After a few seconds, I decide to help. "Oh, here it is, John. Here's your queen. Good job! You know, John, I bet your wife was a queen," I remark, gently stroking his arm.

The unidentified blonde approaches. "Yes, yes, she was. That's my dad," she says, a pool of tears welling in her eyes.

I blink and feel my throat tighten.

"Oh my gosh," I exclaim. "I love your dad. My name is Jeanne. I'm a volunteer here and I just think the world of your dad. Tell me more about him."

"My mom's name was Jean," she says. "She died a few years ago from Alzheimer's and she was extraordinary."

What a divine moment, this opportunity to know more about this gifted man. I can't wait to learn more.

She tells me her name is Laura. She's a flight attendant for a major airline and lives a few hours from the assisted living facility. She tells me her dad was the best dad in the world. He worked as an aeronautical engineer and was a World War II naval veteran. Working on the *USS Laws* during World War II, he was a bona fide hero.

There were four children altogether. John and his wife, Jean, lived a wonderful life in the San Fernando Valley. Given the similarity in our names, I felt it ironic that the children had a dachshund since my family had one when I was growing up. John especially likes visits from his grown son and his dog Chopper.

I'm not surprised to learn that John is in the late stages

of Alzheimer's. I feel so bad for Laura, having watched two amazing parents transformed by the same disease.

Laura is a lot like me. Bubbly and enthusiastic, she holds the hands of many of the residents and talks to them in a soothing voice. "Hi, sweetheart. How are you today? You look good. You're sooo sweet," she coos to John's roommate, Alberto. Pulling him forward, she gives him a gentle kiss on the cheek.

Before the visit ends, we exchange cell phone numbers. Laura grabs my hand and tells me she is so grateful for my visits with her dad. "Thank you, thank you sooo much. I can't tell you how much this means to me." I reassure her that I enjoy doing it, and I just knew her dad was special. Now I understand why.

Two weeks later, a good friend of mine gives me a fabulous idea, "The next time you visit John, why don't you send Laura a text and let her know you saw her dad? I'm sure it would make her day."

I decide to do just that. At the end of my next weekly visit with John, I text Laura, "Just saw your dad today. When I mentioned your name, he beamed."

Within ten seconds she writes back, "Thank you, Jeanne. You're an angel!"

And guess what? I feel like the tallest person in the world. It is a small act of kindness. It is the stuff that Mother Teresa wrote about. It is such an easy thing to do and yet it creates a moment that neither of us will forget. Pure and simple, it's nothing short of magical.

Suddenly, my dream of wanting to be like Lady Diana seems to be coming true, albeit on a much smaller scale. It doesn't matter. I know that I'm making a difference. It's small yet it feels mighty.

Chapter 6

Anybody Wanna Leg?

My younger brother Russell was born without a fully formed foot. Instead, he had a rounded stump with two little toes. His knee and most of his tibia were intact, so if you didn't see him in shorts, you'd never know his foot was missing. My parents wanted to make sure he was independent, so they refused to help him when he fell off his bike or encountered some sort of obstacle typical of childhood.

A doctor suggested that my parents do their best to treat my brother as if he didn't have a disability. "Don't treat him any differently," the doctor suggested. In actuality, my parents DID treat him differently and this had a remarkable impact on his confidence and his independence.

My mother would say, "We didn't help him when he fell off his tricycle. Instead, we gently encouraged him to get back on it and ride again. We wanted him to do just about everything on his own." And just about everything was what he did. From snow skiing to water skiing to an award-winning high school gymnastics performance, there wasn't much Russell couldn't master.

It also made for some comical moments. One day when my brother was about six years old, my mother was at her typical kitchen lookout watching for some neighborhood drama to perk up her routine day, when she suddenly screamed out the window, "Russell, put your leg back on! IT'S NOT A WEAPON!"

My brother was having a disagreement with his neighbor friend JW. JW was convinced Russell couldn't beat him at whiffle ball, a popular sport within our cul-de-sac community of twenty-six children.

Blessed with incredible upper body strength, a decent throwing arm, and a strong sense of confidence, my brother knew better. "I'll show you, JW. I can beat you at anything!"

Within seconds, he pulled off his very expensive and now dangerous artificial limb and shook it wildly over his head with the intention of whacking JW across his body.

We all knew that when my mom screamed, it was time to stop. At the sound of her shrieking, Russell put down his prosthetic leg and immediately came into the house to receive additional admonishment. Meanwhile, little JW ran home to tell his mother about the incident, expecting her to be angry. He was indignant when she started laughing uncontrollably.

Though Russell never again attempted to use his leg as a weapon, he did use it to get laughs on more than one occasion. During a family Thanksgiving dinner, he asked if anybody wanted a leg, and then threw his artificial limb onto the dining room table. The act was received by my aunts, uncles, and cousins with thunderous laughter. This sense of comedic timing was just another reason that Russell was the darling "baby" of the family. Not only was he mechanically inclined and very athletic, he was funny too.

Another time, we were driving to our favorite vacation spot, Ocean City, Maryland, when he decided to become the funny man. Usually the three-hour drive was punctuated by the repeated question, "Are we there yet?" Back in those days, my mother would drive and chain smoke with the windows sealed shut. It made for a rather unpleasant journey.

So my brother took it upon himself to make the ride more interesting. He removed his artificial leg and put it on his knee with the foot toward his face. I can tell you there isn't a contortionist in the world who can make that happen.

My mother happened to glance back and saw the leg on his knee. With her cigarette dangling from her lips, she screamed, "RUSSELL, you stop that immediately. Someone is going to get into an accident!" My older brother and I were reeling with laughter. We loved the type of antics that made my mother frantic.

Russell wasn't all fun and games, though. He could be highly serious sometimes and has always been incredibly brilliant.

Each year, he visited Kernan's Hospital in Baltimore (today known as the University of Maryland Rehabilitation & Orthopaedic Institute), the first orthopedic hospital of its kind in Maryland, operational since 1911. Despite his congenital birth defect, he was born with a functional kneecap, so he walked with a smooth gait. In fact, when he would get fitted for a new leg, the interns were hard pressed to identify which leg was the artificial limb. Nine times out of ten they were wrong.

The orthopedic technicians were amazed and amused that a five-year-old could give them legitimate directions on how to make his new leg. "I don't want the straps. I like it this way. Take them off." His word was final and the leg was made to his specifications.

When he was five, his toes were amputated to give him a

clean stump and allow his artificial leg to fit more comfortably. It was the only time I saw my father cry. I know the phantom pain associated with amputation can be excruciating.

I was seven at the time and felt oddly sad to see Russell's cute little toes disappear forever. I remember telling him so after the surgery. "Russell, I miss your little toes. I liked them. Do you miss them?" He tossed my remarks aside with an annoyance that suggested I was an idiot for even having such thoughts.

My brother went on to graduate from Northeastern University as an electrical engineer and have three beautiful children. Today, we share a collective history rich with color and character. He mimics the many sayings of our mother and our beloved aunt. One of our favorite sayings is "I can't be fooling with that!" It was usually said in response to someone asking them to do something that didn't require much effort.

One time my brother volunteered to wash my aunt's car to which she retorted, "I can't be fooling with that." Attempting a rational explanation, he said, "Aunt Bette, don't you understand, I'm washing YOUR car? It doesn't require anything from you." She retorted that it would involve her pulling supplies out. Russell rolled his eyes in exasperation, knowing there wasn't much point in arguing.

While my brother no longer uses his leg as a weapon or slaps it onto the dinner table, he does continue to make me laugh. And I hear my mom laughing right alongside us.

Chapter 7

Getting Back on Track

After I lost my job in 2008, the severance package sustained me for a year. While I was experimenting with dating, I continued to apply for jobs. I knew it would take at least six to nine months for me to find a career that would be equal to what I had before.

In November 2009, my cousin died suddenly. My severance was set to end that December. I was in full-blown perimenopause and began to experience crippling anxiety. It got so bad I asked my ex-husband to spend nights at my house because I was afraid to go to sleep. Worse yet, I still hadn't found a job and time was running out.

I remember waking up in the middle of the night gripped by fear. *What if I lose my house that I worked so hard to get? Where will Jason and I live? How will I cope?* The anxiety was so bad that I began to understand why someone might contemplate suicide. While I never actually considered it, I understood the feeling. It scared the living hell out of me.

Fortunately, my doctor knew it was chemically related to perimenopause, and he put me on hormone replacement therapy. It was such a relief because I needed to go on interviews and the thought of having a panic attack during an interview was debilitating.

It did the trick, and soon I was back to work. It had taken me fifteen long months to find a career replacement. I took a job as the director of corporate brand marketing for a global manufacturing company. One of my longtime work friends recommended me for the job, and I was so relieved to know we could keep our lives afloat.

When my focus shifted to getting up to speed on my new job, the dating fizzled. I'd given up on ever finding Mr. Right, and I was fine with that. I had a healthy living, great friends, and family who loved me. Plus, Jason was growing up faster than I believed possible.

I was grateful. I was hopeful. I was back to being me.

Gail Is Dying

Dora emails to let me know that Gail has lung cancer and is in hospice care. She doesn't have long. Residents who are critically ill receive in-care hospice services to help them transition to the other world. It's a wonderful way to go out, I think.

I want to talk to Gail before she goes. One of the aides tells me I can go to her room for a personal visit. Approaching her door, I peer in so as not to disturb her. She's asleep, her lips moving as if she's talking to someone. I don't want to wake her.

She looks peaceful, not like my mother looked as she lay dying. She's fortunate. There aren't any tubes connected to her body. She appears to be pain-free. She's in a beautiful, carpeted bedroom full of life and personal mementos, not a cold and impersonal hospital room.

I look at the photos on her wall, carefully examining the aging photographs. I want to understand more about the woman I liked so much. I see her house, the one with the swimming pool. The architecture is interesting, like a castle, but painted red. It suits her personality to a tee.

In one photograph, she grins at the camera, cradling a martini in one hand and holding a cigarette in the other. She told me she never smoked. I'm suddenly sad, realizing so much of her memory was taken, the good, the bad, and the ugly.

Then again, from the photographs, she seems to have had a good life.

In another picture, she is bowling. Bowling? She didn't strike me as a bowler. I saw her more as someone who belonged to a private golf club and enjoyed the game with a number of her friends.

Younger photos of Gail are scattered on the bureau along with photos of her children. Her smile lights up the image. She was pretty. She still is, I think. There's hope for me one day. Beauty really does come from the inside. Once I asked Gail about plastic surgery, so prevalent in California.

"Never. Why would you mess with what God's given you?" Gail chuckled.

"Oh Gail, you are lucky. You are beautiful. Not everyone can be as beautiful as you and me," I laughed.

Gail replied, "Everyone is beautiful, honey."

I will miss her more than I'd like to admit. I have gotten close to her. I want to ask her so many more questions. *What is your secret to happiness? How did you stay married to the same man for all those years? What was your favorite life experience?*

I never get the chance. By December my calendar is filling up with holiday preparations. Gail passes before I can get back and see her. I grieve her loss. I liked her so much. Gail gave me hope. She made me feel young and alive. She made me realize I have so much more to give, so much more to do.

Chapter 8

There Are No Coincidences

*You begin to see the marvelous connections and invisible
threads that connect you from one person to another.*

—Squire Rushnell, *Divine Alignment*

I once read a book called *Divine Alignment,* written by Squire
Rushnell, the author of the bestselling Godwink series. That
book changed my life.

It's all about coincidences that lead us to a new opportunity,
a new relationship, or a new way of thinking.

I wouldn't characterize myself as being extremely religious.
Growing up, I was exposed to Lutheran teachings and I prayed
quite often. As a young adult, I became less religious and more
spiritual, having a strong sense of faith that life's challenges
would somehow work out through prayer and hope. So I was
primed for the message of this book.

One of the stories in *Divine Alignment* is about a woman,
Jane, who wore a POW bracelet in 1971 in honor of a colonel
captured during the war.[3] In 1973, she was watching televi-

---

3   POW bracelets were worn during that time to increase awareness of
POW soldiers. They were usually presented to the former prisoner once they
returned to the US.

sion and saw that the POW had returned from captivity. She shrieked in delight, knowing her prayers had been answered.

In 2010, friends invited Jane and her husband to an Astros game. While she didn't initially want to go, her husband convinced her to, reminding her it wasn't every day a person gets to attend an Astros game.

Reluctantly, she accompanied her husband to the park. She sensed an excitement in the air that made her feel better about her decision. An announcer stepped up to introduce the first pitch, and she was shocked to learn it was being thrown by her POW, the colonel!

Jane shouted, "That's my POW. That's my POW!" She knew she *had* to meet him, only she was quite a distance from home plate and would be stopped numerous times by officials guarding the various sections if she tried to get to him. Still, she was determined to meet him.

Soon after, a camera crew approached her friend and told her she was selected to win $25,000 if an Astros player hit a grand slam in the sixth inning. Seizing the Godwink opportunity, the woman explained her story about wanting to meet the POW with whom she had such a special connection.

The crew's marketing executive shared her excitement, proclaiming that her grandfather was a POW. Before she knew it, Jane was being led past one gatekeeper after another until she was standing before the colonel.

She described how she'd worn his bracelet everywhere—to high school games, to the prom, to church. The colonel told her that while he was in captivity, the guards told him he would die there. She told him she'd prayed for him every night.

She told him, "You are my hero." He replied humbly, "No, you are my *hero.*"

Jane's story and the rest of the book touched me deeply. I was determined to start watching for divine alignment in my circumstances.

Soon after, I began to notice seemingly impossible events happening in my life at just the right time and in ways I never expected. The circumstances just seemed too calibrated to feel like accidents.

I reflected on how things worked out for me at just the right moment in time. When I was laid off from my mortgage job and my severance ran out, another job presented itself just before I was completely out of money.

When I thought I could lose my house after my divorce, I secured a home equity line of credit just before the banks started to shut down all equity (this was during the height of the mortgage meltdown). The funds allowed me to keep my house and pay off my ex-husband.

When I worried about my mother's health and wondered how I would care for her should she become ill (she was in Baltimore and I was in California), she made the move to California. She lived one more year, and I was with her during her last days. I held her hand and told her all the things I needed to in order to make peace.

And then there is the magic of human connections, meeting the right person at just the right time. These moments gave me faith and belief in a higher power that connects us all and gives us what we need—just maybe not when we expect it.

Around the same time I was introduced to *Divine Alignment*, I met a wonderful vivacious woman during jury duty who shared similar life experiences and a shared passion for spirituality. She told me about a book called *E-Squared* by Pam Grout.

The book is about how our thoughts produce energy into

the universe and therefore affect our lives. It's similar to other books on the subject of creating a rich, abundant life, such as *The Secret* by Rhonda Byrne.

Henry Ford said, "Whether you think you can, or you think you can't—you're right." It's that notion of self-fulfilling prophecies: our thoughts control our outcome. I began to recognize how my upbeat, glass-half-full personality affected others. If my mood was upbeat, people picked up on that energy and responded in a positive way. It created more energy in me and often lasted through an entire day.

I worked that "magic" into my senior visits. I began to recognize that I had a special power to bring out joy in people. In return, I received more joy than I ever expected was possible.

Playing and Dancing

E very day is different. Some days, the residents are restless, tired, and unresponsive. Most days, I'm lucky and a few of them will smile and look at me like I'm a long-lost friend. We have spirited conversations fueled by my many questions. I'm convinced they remember me—not my name, of course, but my essence.

During one visit, I run into Laura, John's daughter.

"Laura. How are you? I'm so glad to see you." We embrace.

"Jeanne, glad to see you too. I've been so busy and I'm not feeling well. I want to thank you so much for everything. I received your text messages—I'm sorry I haven't responded."

"I understand," I assure her. "It's no problem."

Laura tosses a beach ball to me, and I take over the game she was playing. I toss it to each resident and ask them questions.

"What's your favorite color?"

"What's your favorite vacation spot?"

"Hurry. Think fast," I challenge them as I toss the ball again.

John is alert. I tell Laura how good he looks and how much I love him.

Overhearing me, John gives me his big, gorgeous grin.

"John, I keep telling you, they don't make them like you anymore. I keep trying to get a man. I just can't find one like you."

Nona giggles at this. Her giggle is soft and sweet, matching her beautiful smile. When I look at her, I just know she loves to smile and it comes easy for her.

"What is your dog's name again?" she asks.

Wow, she remembers?

This validates my theory. They do remember me, or at least they get a warm, strong feeling when they see me. It doesn't matter. What matters is that I make them smile. I thrive on the smiles. I thrive on the moments with these sweet souls.

Laura tells her dad that she needs to leave and that I will be taking over.

"You aren't coming back," he says.

I'm not sure whether it's a statement or a question. It breaks my heart. He thinks she's not coming back.

"I'm definitely coming back, Dad. I'll be here in two weeks," Laura tells him, tears welling in her eyes. "I love you, Daddy." She reaches over to kiss him and rubs his arm before turning to leave.

I know she hates leaving him. It's not that this is such a bad place. I'm certain she hates knowing he is alone, without family, and living in confusion, fear, and forgetfulness. It must be hard knowing she can't rescue him from it.

These souls are lost and without a map. It can be excruciating to watch. It's like leaving your child at kindergarten for the first time. You walk out in the middle of a hysterical crying fit. You know your child will be okay, but for the moment, your heart is aching. It takes everything in your will not to stay and protect the one you love the most.

I bat the beach ball back to John and he eagerly tosses it back. "He'll be fine," I tell Laura. She hugs me and thanks me again.

"Hey, everyone, how aaaarrrrrre you?" I call when attention lags. "I'm still hanging in there. Hoping to find a man. I can't seem to get a man interested in me. What's up with that?"

Marcus, the aide says, "I don't know why. I'm sure that's not true. From where I stand, you have it all." Marcus is a handsome black man in his late twenties. I love watching him with the residents; you can tell he cares about making them comfortable. I marvel at his gentleness and his kind soul, given his youth. I take his compliments as a mother would take a son's.

"You need glasses, Marcus," I respond.

"I'm too young to need glasses," he says and moves on to help a resident to her hair appointment.

I toss the beach ball to Jillian and ask her about her secret to living. She's 100 now and still on top of her game.

"Jillian, did you smoke or drink?" I ask.

"Oh yes, many years ago, I smoked. I drank wine and bourbon."

"The hard stuff? Wow, Jillian, it gives me hope. I wanna be as sexy as you when I turn 100."

That sends Nona into another fit of giggles.

Another resident, Drew, insists out of the blue that we "get this thing going."

"What thing going?" I ask.

"Getting people together," he says. He gestures with his fingers to form a circle of imaginary people. I sense he was a no-nonsense guy in his time.

"You either do it or get out!" he exclaims.

Something about this exchange halts me. I'm humbled by Drew's strength. Here's a very principled man who did things the right way, and now his words are utter nonsense to anyone who doesn't know better. This might be me one day. I might be the person who talks utter nonsense. The thought gives me a lump in my throat.

I treat him with kindness and do the best I can to acknowledge the importance of his words. "That's right, Drew," I say, "either do it the right way or don't do it at all. That's what I tell my son."

He nods in approval and tells me we must start now. I redirect by saying we'll have a conversation for now and then it will be time for lunch. He's not satisfied and mutters something under his breath about people not understanding how to get things done.

Meanwhile, a motion across the room captures my attention. Marion is dancing with Marty. They are not a couple, yet they act as if they have been married for years. Both are equally flirtatious, as if they are teenagers getting ready to attend their first prom. He picks her up gently from the sofa and asks her to dance with him, putting his arms delicately around her. They step slowly from side to side. I hope Marion is somewhere else in time, somewhere beautiful, swaying to lovely music, surrounded by gorgeous scenery, and held in the arms of someone she loves. This is her moment.

Several days later, I have a dream. A younger man moves toward me and takes my hand. He asks me to dance. I say, "No, I can't dance." I sense I have a physical condition that renders me unable to move. Despite my firm answer, he takes me in his arms and twirls me about. I feel alive, euphoric. The energy surrounding me is surreal. It's an indescribable feeling of light, almost like being in love. When I wake, I analyze the dream. Is that how Marion feels when Marty dances with her? I sure hope so.

Chapter 9

A New Man for My Mom

*I believe that everything happens for a reason. People change
so that you can learn to let go, things go wrong so that you
appreciate them when they're right, you believe lies so you
eventually learn to trust no one but yourself, and sometimes
good things fall apart so better things can fall together.*

—Marilyn Monroe

After the death of my dad, my mom struggled to keep from feeling overwhelmed. At thirty-nine, she was alone with three small children from ages seven to thirteen. Her grief took many forms: anger, resentment, and despair. To get by, she eventually turned to self-medication.

It was the seventies, and the thought of popping pills to manage grief was unconscionable. Only later, as a young adult, did I learn exactly how much she drank. Yet, she functioned, if you could call it that. I don't recall seeing my mother "drunk" or slurring her words. She cooked dinner almost every night, she modeled incredible morality and tolerance, and she made sure we had everything we needed and then some.

I remember her telling me right after my dad's death that she thought she had money, so she spent a lot of it taking us on nice vacations, including a three-night cruise to the Bahamas. I guess along with her drinking habit, spending money she didn't have was a way to cope.

I remember her reading a book called *God, But I'm Bored!* It was a small, tidy paperback with dog-eared pages that she kept on her nightstand. In hindsight, it looks like a symbol of the black hole that would become her life. I don't think my mother ever got over my dad's death—she just learned to live with it.

She once told me that a fortune teller who read her palm said she would never meet another man to match the one she lost. My father, Dick, WAS the love of her life. I suppose this fortune reader gave her permission to continue living her life without love. My mom told me more than once that she didn't want to deal with another man. "I don't want to wash someone's socks, take care of him when he's sick, deal with all that crap!" She'd never felt that way dealing with my father's stuff.

She felt sorry for women who needed a man to complete them. My mom had a beautiful and vivacious girlfriend who felt this way, and she too lost her husband. Carol was in her early forties when she became a widow, and she didn't want to be alone. Sharply dressed with a smart chic cut and stunning blue-green eyes, Carol was always in the company of a boyfriend. Some of them were not quite right. A few were loud and obnoxious. A few my mother couldn't stand.

As a young girl, I heard my mother's message loud and clear: she was not going to settle. That didn't stop her from dating periodically, as she often met men through her piano-playing gigs at various hotel venues or restaurants. One such man that captured her attention was an architect named Arthur.

They met at the downtown Baltimore Hilton Hotel. He would stop by after work and sit down with a Manhattan to watch my mom play and sing her heart out. She would coo Nat King Cole's romantic ballad *Embraceable You* in her rusty cigarette voice.

A busty platinum blonde, she filled a room with her presence and her talent. She wore all the latest designer fads from the seventies, including flowing polyester tops that were intended to be worn braless.

Mesmerized by her makeup routine, I would often stare at her reflection in the mirror as she carefully applied her blue eyeshadow, black liner, and rich coral lipstick. One particular evening as she was readying herself for work, she wore that top without a bra.

I exclaimed with exasperation and anxiety, "You're not going to wear that, are you?"

"I most certainly am," she retorted, smug and determined. I remember battling with her and quite possibly resorting to cries of protest. I was embarrassed that she would wear such a thing in public. I could see her huge nipples breathing through the top and I was ashamed of her.

That was about a year or two after my father's death. She needed to feel sexy and alive, even if it meant going to battle with a very upset eleven-year-old daughter on a daily basis. She went out without a bra, feeling sexy and free.

Arthur soon became a frequent visitor. I remember noticing how my mother's voice was different when she spoke to him over the phone. Typically boisterous and loud, my mother answered in some sort of alien voice that seemed on the verge of smoldering sultriness.

Annoyed by her new fake-sounding voice, I asked, "Why are you talking like that?" She pretended not to understand what I was talking about.

Arthur finally came to the house to meet the children of this enchanting woman of many talents. I liked him. He was tall and handsome, soft spoken, and very kind. He seemed very interested in me and asked me a lot of questions about what I enjoyed doing.

They would retreat to the basement to "talk," my mother requesting privacy from each of her children. Of course, I was certain to interrupt, looking for much needed fatherly attention only to be greeted by Arthur with an amused grin.

All of a sudden and without warning, Arthur stopped coming by the house. My mother remained silent and somber about it. I soon learned that Arthur had broken it off. My mother never shed one tear, though I know for sure she had real feelings for him.

Only years later did my mother explain that Arthur was married and felt very conflicted about his relationship with my mother. He and his wife were separated, and their marriage was practically over. Even though my mom's relationship with Arthur ended before it really began, it chased away the grief she had over my father's death. In other words, it served a very great purpose.

She told me that my grandmother and my aunts had been supportive because it was the first time my mother had seemed genuinely happy again.

Sometimes people come into our lives for a short season. There is a reason and a purpose, and though it may prove painful to cut ties, we gain something from the relationship. That was the case for my mother and Arthur.

My mother was the kind of woman who lived with a solid moral compass yet sometimes saw the gray in the world. I loved that she was not judgmental, especially when things weren't what they appeared to be. As a musician, her views were very contemporary. She was a feminist before her time, believing that women could manage a career and a family. She had friends from all walks of life and even friends who lived non-conventional lifestyles.

I liked that my mother taught me understanding and depth. Swirling her cigarette about like Bette Davis in a dramatic black-and-white movie, she would often say, "Conversation should have depth and substance. I want to know what makes a person tick. I want to know about them and how they view the world." If she felt someone didn't have depth, they were an absolute bore. It didn't matter if they were extroverted or introverted, it was all about having meaningful conversation.

As the years went by, the men in my mother's life disappeared as quickly as they entered. Soon she showed no interest whatsoever in dating, and by her late forties she was done with men.

As for me, I was still interested in men in my forties. I often wondered what caused my mother to shut down, though I did understand why she decided not to marry again. I had pretty much decided I wouldn't marry again either.

The universe had other plans for me, though. Or just maybe that was Shirley's doing.

Chapter 10

Starting a New Chapter

Years passed, and I was still visiting my friends at the assisted living center. I'd discovered so much since I'd started visiting old people in 2009. Not to mention I was closing the gap on being considered an "older" person myself.

The world was changing A LOT. It seemed with every passing year our collective society was becoming more divided. There was so much discord and hate. And it's hard to run away from it when we're so digitally connected to the world's events and strife.

I saw alienation and loneliness all around me. Loneliness is fixable. Hate not so much. I chose to visit old people because I knew for a few hours each week I could banish their loneliness. The way their eyes lit up, the twinkling smiles buried under a sea of wrinkles, the touch of their bony, overworked fingers—it captivated me to use my power of compassion for transformative magic.

We all have the "magic." We just don't always know how to tap into it, or we're too lazy to expend the energy. It takes energy to "move" people. It's not just about moving your mouth—it requires a good deal of physical stamina to be joyful, optimistic, and hopeful even when you don't feel like it.

I love the saying, "Fake it till you feel it." It's surprising how people can either suck all of our energy or give us more. Haven't you ever met someone who made you so tired that you needed a three-hour nap just to recover? Conversely, haven't you met those energy givers who have a way of turning your day around? That's who I want to be, and I want to inspire others to be that person too.

So how can we all do this? Don't give up. Focus on the things you can do to make the world a better place. Little acts of kindness cost nothing and the return on investment is more than you can ever imagine possible.

I know. Love brought me love. I really believe that. As I have given love and believed that I'm lovable, the universe has reached out and given me exactly what I was looking for.

It took me a long time to learn this lesson, more than half my lifetime. So now I have a lot more to say and so much more to do. Because the world really needs people who care.

In August of 2011, I found myself unemployed AGAIN after working for a global manufacturing company for approximately fifteen months. I was laid off and given a few months' severance. This time I was actually relieved because I wasn't a cultural fit and felt miserable.

In between, I did some freelance work. I was fortunate to begin consulting with a financial services company and developed a strong bond with the president. He liked me enough that he agreed to allow me to work remotely (the company was based in Bellevue, Washington) and travel periodically to the home office for key meetings. I accepted a full-time position working remotely in November of 2012.

Little did I know that things would soon change. And in bigger ways than I thought possible.

After all, I was adamant, if not arrogant, I would *never* leave Southern California for rainy, depressing Seattle. I had a beautiful home in Simi Valley located right down the street from the gorgeous Ronald Reagan Library. I had an eighteen-year-old son nowhere near ready for independence or college, and two very pampered Doxie mixes who enjoyed a "stay-at-home mom." Plus, I had a multitude of girlfriends who actually preferred my company, even when it meant giving up time with their husbands or boyfriends. Frankly, I thought I had it all.

I loved my job. It provided the perfect balance. I could work from home and there was just the right mix of travel peppered in to keep me stimulated. I would brag to my family and friends about how lucky I was to have a job that allowed me to work remotely.

I could be productive, eliminate the California commutes that cause nervous breakdowns, and get dinner on the table at a decent time. I loathed making dinners after a long day at the office. Okay, truth be told, I hated making dinner at all.

The business travel was fabulous and required no cooking. To my surprise, I found myself actually liking Seattle, even when it rained. There was something extraordinarily clean and beautiful about the place. Plus, it's surrounded by water, and I've always had a spiritual connection to water.

While in the Bellevue office, I was able to charm everyone with my "sunny disposition," a characteristic common to people who live in places with more than 300 days of sunshine. Why wouldn't I be happy, perky, and humorous when I had the best of all worlds?

After my business day was complete, it wasn't unusual for me to head to a local restaurant with a nice bar to have a light dinner and a green apple martini. My mother once said that she had never met a bar stool that wasn't comfortable. I guess I follow in her footsteps.

As a seasoned female business traveler, I was comfortable going out alone. I never suspected people stared at me and thought, *What's up with her? She looks so pathetic sitting there alone.* I actually preferred dining out as opposed to eating alone in my hotel room. Thanks to my mother, I felt attractive, confident, and completely at ease making conversation with strangers. And, boy, did I have some interesting conversations.

I've flirted all my life. I especially enjoyed flirting once I'd made up my mind that I was content with my single life—it was a harmless way to connect with the opposite sex without commitment. It kept me from accumulating any unnecessary baggage that might prove too heavy for me to carry.

At the time, I thought almost all men had some amount of baggage. Since I had a *fixer* personality, I knew I would carry more than my share, which would inevitably take its toll on my health in the form of stress or anxiety. Neither was an option for me.

So I safely flirted. It wasn't uncommon for me to meet a few single men during my evenings out having dinner. I admit there were times when I wondered if a man I met might be "the one." Even in my glorious contentment, I had a mustard seed of faith that I could find someone in the city of Seattle who would be different than the men I met in California.

Many of these conversations left me disenchanted. The deal killers were: "I hate my ex-wife. She never understood me." NEXT. "I'm in between jobs right now. It's only been two years and I have a few things lined up." NEXT. "I think you're drop-dead gorgeous, and we really need to take advantage of this magic because it doesn't hit very often." The man who said this suggested I meet him at his hotel room. Even if he had a sexy English accent, it was NEXT.

One night, I met a very nice divorcee willing to have a deeper conversation with me about the characteristics I'd need from the "ideal" mate. I was of the opinion that writing out your life goals was the key to achieving them. I spent a lot of years writing down my short-term and long-term goals, many of which came true for me. Ironically, I never got around to writing a list of characteristics I wanted in a romantic suitor. I thought about it a lot and knew women who had written down exactly what they wanted in a mate and then met their perfect match. Most likely, I wasn't ready. I didn't make it a priority until someone did it for me.

I told this divorcee every single attribute I could think of for the kind of man who would hold the keys to my heart. The list included everything from having a healthy sense of humor to a credit score over 700, seriously.

He wrote it all down and then handed me the list and told me to keep it. I did and I still have it.

Eight months later, the man with all of the qualities on that list (well, almost everything) walked into my life.

Rachel

Rachel is truly the odd man out. She's the only one in the group who's "awake" yet non-responsive to my questions. I can count on her to give me a half-hearted smile and that's about it. I guess that will have to be enough for now.

Honey-gold hair falls shoulder-length around her delicate eyes. She must have been very pretty in her day. Rachel's eyes are as blue as Paul Newman's, and her lips are always tightly pursed as if to say, "Just leave me alone."

There's a bitterness about her demeanor. What happened to her in life to make her put her guard up? Maybe her husband died prematurely. Perhaps she lost a child. I have no way of knowing. She's a complete mystery to me.

The first time we met, I asked her one of my typical questions. "Rachel, what is your favorite vacation spot?" She looked annoyed, glaring at me. She carefully raised her index finger, wagging it back and forth with an emphatic, "NO."

Message received. She didn't want to talk to me.

After that first exchange, I haven't pressed her. I don't want to make her uncomfortable by asking unwanted questions. It's hard enough to be in a strange land without having some other stranger make it more unbearable.

Still, I can't bring myself to ignore her. Whenever possible, I look into her eyes and pay special attention to her even when I know she won't participate. I smile at her a lot. I laugh at my own jokes. Every now and then, I see her chuckle. It makes me want to find more ways to amuse her.

With every passing week, Rachel's eyes light up more and more when I enter the room. Maybe I'm earning her respect by honoring her boundary. That's another reason I think these residents know me even if they can't remember me in the usual sense. When I walk into the room and chirp my larger-than-life "HELLO," I see and feel an incredible reaction. Maybe my familiar tone and essence makes a mark in the recesses of the subconscious.

This week, as I'm getting ready to leave after my usual visit, I say my goodbyes and let the residents know that I'll return. Walking over to some of my favorites, I stroke an arm, give a hug, or squeeze a hand. I walk over to say goodbye to Rachel.

"Rachel, it was so good to see you again. I hope you feel okay today."

I wait for the expected silence. She surprises me by taking my hand in hers and touching it to her lips.

"I love you," she whispers. "You are so cute."

I'm at once ecstatic and emotional. This is the first time Rachel has truly acknowledged me. A tear forms in the corner of my eye and a lump clogs my throat.

"Why, thank you so much, Rachel. This means so much coming from you, my little shy flower. I love you too, darling."

I feel like Rudolph, prancing and shouting, "She likes me, she likes me!" when Clarisse professes her love. I hold her hand and drink in the delight of that moment. She remembers me. Yep, she sure does.

Chapter 11

Are You Lovable?

We are powerfully imprisoned by the terms in which we have been conducted to think.

—Buckminster Fuller, American inventor and futurist

In 2014, after reading *E-Squared*, I began to question some of the "tapes" that I replayed both in conversations with close girlfriends and in my own head. I recognized that one of my "tapes" was convincing myself I was happier and better off single and that, for the most part, men were selfish creatures.

I knew that I was unwilling to "settle" for any man who would not complement me. Not to mention that it was highly unlikely that I'd ever meet the man who had all the qualities on my list.

I also knew that if I were to commit to someone with even a little baggage, I would own it entirely. This meant I'd feel responsible for every mistake or misdeed this man would ever make. Just as a mother may feel responsible for the sins of her children, I'd take ownership of any fatal flaws even if they weren't mine to own in the first place. Completely irrational, right?

I'm not quite sure why I have this tendency to own other

people's problems. I guess you could say I love too much or I'm codependent, or I'm just wacky. Whatever the case, I was self-aware, adored self-analysis even to the point of paralysis, and knew exactly what made me tick.

So if you believe in self-fulfilling prophecies, I was all set up to live a life alone, except for a little voice inside my head asking, "What makes you think you're unlovable?" WOW. That sure stopped me in my tracks. Could all this tape-playing be a disguise for a belief that I couldn't find someone who could love me and believe I was worthy of love? NOW WAIT JUST A MINUTE.

I started taking long walks in my beautiful Simi Valley planned community to look for the beauty around me and to meditate. Now before you dismiss me, consider the alternative. What good is it doing you to have negative thoughts? Or, as Dr. Phil likes to say, "How's that working for you?" That's one of my favorite lines, by the way.

My tape was negative. *I don't need a man. I don't need the baggage. I'm not going to settle.* Blah, blah, blah, blah.

I began to answer my own inner question: *Do you believe you're not lovable? If so, why?* You seem to choose men who are unattainable or possess the very characteristics you don't want. *Why do you do that?* Well, I guess I don't want to get hurt. It's easier to self-sabotage and prove I'm correct in the first place.

So what if I change my tape? What might happen? What do I have to lose by trying a little positive thinking?

So in January of 2014 I started changing my tape. It went something like this: *I'm lovable. I know I will find love. I deserve to be loved. Love is here.*

Four months later, love would present itself.

Chapter 12

Meeting Julie

In April of 2014, I worked my company's sales incentive event at the exquisite Pelican Hill Resort in Newport Beach, California. The venue is spectacular. Practically palatial with its 2,000-square-foot rooms, bigger than most people's homes, it sits high above the Palisades bluff with panoramic views overlooking the Pacific Ocean.

The building itself is beautiful too, built in Palladian architectural style. Boasting the world's largest circular pool, it's the ideal destination for group gatherings, weddings, or a romantic rendezvous.

During the event, I met Julie, my new boss's wife. I had begun reporting to my boss, Darren, in September of 2013 after transitioning from reporting to the president. He was a difficult man to read at first, and I was just sorting out my relationship with him when I fell in love with his wife.

Julie, a dark-haired Irish beauty with stunning blue-green eyes, captivated my attention right away. She was down-to-earth, touchy-feely expressive, with a hearty sense of humor. As mothers of grown sons, we related about how challenging parenting can be.

There was nothing pretentious about her. Julie was straight

to the point, and you knew where you stood with her. She really liked me.

I decided to be real with her and in return she was real with me. I found myself telling her my entire life story—and she listened! We talked about my divorce, alimony, and my eighteen-year-old son, who was probably having a party at the house right about now. I talked to her about my not-so-lucky dating adventures with men. I joked that I couldn't attract a man on life support.

Then I dared to ask, "Do you have any friends I could date in Seattle?" I was half-serious. At least, I think I was.

She paused for a few seconds while she considered my question. I could tell she was giving it serious thought. She tilted her head and looked out into the distance, scanning her brain for any single men that might be a match for my wit and personality.

After what seemed to be a minute or two, Julie said, "Yes, I know somebody. Our friend Joe!" She seemed really pleased with herself. I'm sure that finding a "match" for a fifty-three-year-old woman she'd just met couldn't have been easy. She really had to work her mental rolodex because, as I would learn later, Julie and Darren had more friends than most people have in a lifetime. And most of them were married.

Julie couldn't stop saying enough about Joe. Her eyes sparkled when she talked about him. She told me he is the kindest, nicest guy you could ever meet. *So what's wrong with him?* She said he was their "best friend" and everyone who ever met him liked him immediately.

Julie told me she had never heard him speak a negative word about his ex-wife. This was extremely important to me; I was always turned off by men who seemed to enjoy describing their ex-wives as horrible people or "bitches." I always thought if they could talk that way about someone they once loved, how quickly would they turn on me?

I was intrigued about Joe, this man with the likeable personality, hand-picked by Julie. I wondered if there might possibly be a connection and if I would even find him attractive. At the same time, I worried about him being my boss's best friend. *Probably not a great career move.*

Mrs. Magoo

M iriam looks like a female Mr. Magoo. Quincy Magoo is a cartoon character made famous by the actor Jim Backus back in the 1960s. The cartoon character is a bald, short-statured retiree who gets into crazy situations based on his failing eyesight and his inability to admit to problems. He has a bulbous nose and very squinty eyes.

Miriam has squinty eyes and always looks troubled. Framing her Magoo-like face are deep frown lines that make her look like she's constantly in pain. She paces a lot and doesn't stay long in the common room. I don't take it personally.

I discover that Miriam was a laboratory technician who wanted to be doctor. She didn't pursue her doctorate because "it was too much money." *What a shame to know what you want out of life and not have the means to pursue it.* Few even know what they want. To know and to be denied must be very difficult.

Miriam grew up with three brothers. "I learned to be tough," she quips in an acerbic tone reminiscent of Popeye the Sailor Man. "They were always chasing me and trying to beat me up. I climbed trees, I threw rocks, and I loved it."

I feel sad when she tells me she went on to marry an abusive alcoholic. A working professional with children of her own, Miriam had to put up with that too? I hate the thought of it. Despite the abuse, she stayed in her marriage.

Women did that back then—stayed in the marriage even

when their husband was abusive or indifferent. I'm lucky I didn't have to stay. I loved my husband. Still, I wasn't happy. Unhappy people make for unhappy parents, unhappy friends, and unhappy souls. Pretty soon, the stress takes its toll. I wonder if Mrs. Magoo's dementia was brought on by her abusive husband. I once read a study done at UC Irvine concluding that stress hormones can exacerbate the formation of brain lesions seen in Alzheimer's patients.

Whatever unhappy circumstances led Miriam to her destiny of confusion and pacing, I determine not to follow the same path. I want to find my way through life by enriching the lives of others. They feel better. I feel better. We all live longer, more joyful lives.

Chapter 13

Who Knows, Stranger Things Have Happened

A week or two after returning home from the Pelican Hill Resort that April, Darren texted me. *Julie is really talking you up to our friend Joe. She can't stop talking about you.* AWKWARD.

I was a little stunned. I mean, my boss was texting me about my love life, or lack thereof. How was I to respond? *Oh great, here's my photo. Show your friend.* WEIRD. Besides, I'd already googled this Joe character and didn't like what I saw.

The only photo of Joe I could find on the internet was of him holding a HUGE dead fish! The photo was taken from a very unflattering angle that gave him a thick neck and very red face. His white hair was like a halo around his head, and he was wearing a YELLOW SHIRT. No one looks good in yellow.

I thought to myself, *NO way. This is the guy you want to fix me up with, this fisherman who likes to kill big creatures from the sea?*

Suddenly a voice inside me I had no idea was there said, "Who knows? This could be the guy. You can't tell from a picture. Stranger things have happened."

So now I had to respond to Darren's text with something

clever, witty, and noncommittal. After all, I was fairly certain I did NOT want to be hooked up with Mr. Chicken of the Sea.

(Joe would later brag that this was no "mere" fish. It was a 90-pound bluefin tuna. I guess this is the Cadillac of fish. To me, it's just a slimy, unfortunate creature).

I chose to respond with wit. *Ha. Ha. I'll pay her later. She's wonderful, your wife.* I hoped that would shut it all down.

~

Months went by and I didn't give Joe another thought. At one point, Darren mentioned they co-owned a cabin in the Cascade Mountains with Joe. Darren and Julie occupied the bigger part of the cabin, which was situated on the Wenatchee River, and took their children there to enjoy weekends full of skiing, sledding, river rafting, outdoor movies, game nights, and s'mores by a roaring outdoor fire.

Darren showed me a picture of the cabin and pointed to the mother-in-law suite. "This is where Joe stays." Something about the way he showed me "where Joe stays" made me think Joe was the maintenance man for the cabin. So now I was even more convinced that Joe was not the man for me! I was not a mail-order bride seeking to reside in a log cabin in the middle of nowhere with a handyman. I'm way too high maintenance for that. No pun intended.

I later found out that Joe is an IT director and NOT the cabin's maintenance man. Still, I was not interested in the least! I must admit I was a little too fixated on making sure the physical chemistry was right.

Four months after the sales event at the Pelican Hill Resort, Darren asked me to fly out to Seattle for a business trip. He suggested I stay over the weekend so we could all attend a ZZ Top concert at the Chateau Ste. Michelle Winery.

Located in Woodinville, Washington, the Chateau is Washington State's oldest winery. In the spring and summer months, the Chateau hosts various entertainers in their amphitheater, where guests sprawl on blankets with picnic baskets for an evening of music under the stars. Guests can purchase a nice bottle of wine or two from the winery.

As an afterthought, Darren said, "Oh and, by the way, Joe is coming too."

What? I heard the sound of a vinyl record being scratched. I was in a real predicament. I was being invited to a concert by my BOSS, who would be bringing his friend, the maintenance man, just for grins and giggles.

So what did I do? I called my best friend, Janet, to complain. Janet is my person. Whatever ails me, she's the one who always has my best interests at heart. Friends for more than forty years, we go way back.

Janet told me to stop worrying and go to the concert. At the very least, I might meet a friend. She said you never know what life will bring, and I should just go and have a good time.

"Well, alright. I'll go," I said, sighing like Eeyore. "But I don't have to be happy about it."

I booked my travel sometime late July and decided to keep my promise to Janet. I would go to the concert after all. I was certain I wasn't going to be attracted to Joe, and I decided he wasn't going to be attracted to me.

Chapter 14

The Pedestal Effect

When my father died, my mother would speak about him as if he were a knight in shining armor. Like many people who experience grief, she had a tendency to glorify the deceased and remember only the good qualities.

My mother described their love affair as passionate, stormy, affectionate, respectful, and remarkably different than most married couples. My mom was a twenty-five-year-old buxom blonde in 1956 when she met my dad. He was a traveling sax musician trying to drum up business when he walked into a Baltimore nightclub where my mother was working.

My mother played piano as part of a trio with her best friend, Kelly, who played the bass, and a drummer whose name I cannot recollect. Spotting a photo of the trio, my father was initially attracted to Kelly. That changed when he walked into the club.

My mother was playing and singing a ballad standard. There she was in her velvet evening gown, sporting rich red lipstick and platinum hair, crooning in her smoky voice and giving it all she had at the keyboard. They made eye contact. He was hooked.

After the set, he approached her and insisted she go on a

date with him. My mother told me he went so far as to playfully swing his key in her face to suggest they leave the bar and go to his hotel room. I remember thinking, *Wow, my dad was quite the player* (and I don't mean a saxophone player)!

At the time, my mother was already involved with another man—Kenny the radio station executive, who had been dating my mother for two years. He loved my mother, yet there was something about her that prevented him from taking that next step. In the fifties, people didn't live together. They got married.

My mother would say, "Because I was a musician, Kenny didn't feel I was 'wife material.'" It was a mistake that Kenny later regretted. My mother met Kenny when her first husband was deployed in Germany and she was "separated." That's what she told me to justify the fact that she met and dated someone else while she was married.

Her first husband didn't care for her musicianship. When she purchased a fur stole with the money she made playing music, he broke down in tears. She found the display of emotion weak and utterly repulsive, an effeminate reaction to her independence that marked the beginning of the end. It also marked the beginning of her relationship with Kenny.

My dad wasn't taking no for an answer and my mother wasn't interested in the slightest. On more than one occasion she protested, "I'm in love with someone else. I'm NOT interested." He continued to show up night after night.

Finally, his persistence paid off. Apparently, persistence was a sexy quality my mother appreciated. She agreed to go out with him. That was the beginning of the pedestal effect.

There was no doubt about it, my mom was in love with two men at the same time. She believed that you could be in two places at once. That didn't always serve her well, though. One time, when my father caught her out with Kenny, he pulled Kenny's hat down over his head. OUCH.

My dad walked away and my mother chased after him. "Why in the hell did you have to do that? That wasn't necessary." Oh, the drama between those two. I suspect that drama was the very thing that connected them like a north and south pole magnet.

Eventually, my mom chose my dad. His persistence, his character, their shared love of music, and his unconditional passion and love created a romance that would stand the test of time.

In the middle of a marital separation himself, my dad went back and forth between Providence, Rhode Island, and the entire east coast to find music work, any work. His plan was to take my mother to Las Vegas, find music work (which they did), get a quickie divorce, and then marry her and live happily ever after.

"Jeanne, your dad thought I was nearly perfect. He thought I was beautiful. He loved the way I dressed. He thought I was the best piano player, the best cook, the best mother. He put me on a pedestal."

That pedestal shaped how I looked at men. It affected my entire life, from what I looked for in a man to my unabashed love of compliments. I wanted to be on that pedestal. I wanted all those compliments. I wanted to be chased and courted. I wanted all that exquisite drama.

Once I found that drama, I saw it wasn't all it was cracked up to be. I decided the pedestal effect didn't exist. That is, until I met Joe.

Chapter 15

The Blind Date

In August of that year, my flight to Seattle went without a hitch, and I checked into my local Residence Inn to prepare to attend the ZZ Top concert and meet Joe the Fisherman.

Darren suggested I drive to his home in Woodinville, near the concert venue. From there we'd make the five-minute drive to pick up Joe at his home in Redmond.

While we took the short drive to pick up Joe, I enjoyed my reunion with Julie. She gushed about how wonderful the summer concerts were and gabbed about their wonderful friend Joe.

When we arrived at Joe's home, he stood outside waiting for us. I noticed that he was more attractive than in the photo I'd seen. I got out of the car and approached him.

"Nice to meet you, Joe. I've heard a lot of great things about you."

He flashed me an incredible smile complete with dimples. When he shook my hand, he chuckled and said, "Yeah, they're all lies."

I couldn't help staring at his perfectly straight white teeth and those incredible dimples. *His firm handshake would impress my mother*, I thought. She always said how important a strong grip was and how it defined a person's character. In her view, a weak handshake was emasculating.

His huge hand was warm, and his grin was captivating.

Wow, he's kind of cute. I immediately felt intrigued by his presence and masculinity; it made me feel comfortable. While I found him physically attractive, I was more attracted to his personality and the way he presented himself to the world.

He stood about six feet tall, had a bit of weight around his middle, and sported a beautiful crop of white wavy hair. His blue-green eyes, light skin, and freckles—all Irish traits—made him all the more attractive to me.

Darren thought it would be a good idea for Joe to show me inside his house, which he'd purchased in January of 2014 and was renovating. Joe agreed and ushered me inside.

It was a modest home by most accounts, with a combined family-dining great room that looked out on a cornucopia of flowering plants. It was the masterpiece of the home, a horti-culturist's dream.

The great room was warm, open, and dare I say clean. I was impressed that a fifty-four-year-old single guy occupied this space. I noticed a wooden playhouse with a decorative "clubhouse" placard in the yard.

"Joe, I see you have a clubhouse. Do you have grandchildren?"

"No, I'm just a swinger," he said and chuckled at me.

I laughed at his bold and bodacious sense of humor. *Okay, this is a guy I can like!*

Renovations were well underway upstairs. Joe shared his progress on the two new master bathrooms and the exposed wood flooring that would require all new nails to eliminate the squeaking. It was clear that Joe was doing all the improvements himself.

Hmm, a man who knows his way around power tools. Now THAT IS SEXY.

After the tour, we were back in the car and heading to the concert venue, about five minutes from Joe's house. We parked and pulled a plethora of picnic items from the car. I'd never seen such a lavish collection, from collapsible tables to the finest in melamine dishes to the retractable zero gravity chairs. This group of friends had the picnic experience dialed in!

Finding a spot on the grounds of the Chateau, we unpacked our ultimate ensemble. Joe and I started talking about the concert experience, and Darren was excited to have me try his smoked salmon, even though I noted I was not much of a fish lover.

Joe quickly won me over with his kindness. He was easy to talk to and an attentive listener. As he attempted to get out of the zero gravity chair, very low to the ground, he laughed and said, "It's getting harder and harder each year to get up off these chairs." I enjoyed his quick wit.

As he politely excused himself for the porta-potty, I looked at Julie. "I really like your friend."

She smiled. "I can only tell you that he is one of the few people that I can't find anything negative to say about. He always finds the good in people. We have been friends for years. He is our best friend."

The conversation flowed easily throughout the evening, and Julie later told me it was as if no one was there except for Joe and me. She would affectionately say, "There was no one in the room." Joe and I had a special connection, and it felt like we'd known each other for years. It was friendly and upbeat. I didn't see a single red flag.

He even escorted me to the porta-potties and waited for me

like a classy gentleman, guiding me back to our picnic station. I did what any needy woman seeking validation would do and asked if he would take a picture with me. As I stood beside him to take the photo, I snuggled under his arm and burrowed into his chest, feeling extremely comfortable with this closeness. He put his arm around me and squeezed me in closer, telling Julie to take her time with the camera. I giggled and enjoyed every bit of his flirtatious attention.

Later I texted our picture to a few girlfriends and asked, "What do you think?" One of my girlfriends texted back, "If you don't want him, I'll take him." That was all I needed to hear.

I don't remember much of the concert. I remember how special Joe made me feel and how comfortable I was in his presence.

After Darren realized we had a connection, he decided I would come to his house for dinner with all of them that Tuesday for my favorite cut of beef, ribeye. This time there was no question about whether I would attend.

Before the evening was over, I hinted to Joe that I was planning on spending Sunday in Kirkland, a quaint waterfront town and the original home of the Seattle Seahawks. I was hoping he would offer to accompany me, and I was careful not to say so outright. Instead I took his cell phone number so I could text him our photos and ensure he had my contact information.

That evening I texted our photos and told him I'd really enjoyed meeting him. I received a noncommittal text back that he'd enjoyed the evening too. I went to sleep that night wondering what was to come and not sure whether I wanted anything to come of it or not.

Joan, the Lone Wolf

*I guess I'm pretty much of a lone wolf. I don't say I don't like
people at all but, to tell you the truth, I only like it then if I have
a chance to look deep into their hearts and their minds.*

—Bela Lugosi

Joan is different from the others. It puzzles me why she is
on the Recollections side. One day I ask Dora.

"Dora, Joan doesn't seem to suffer from memory problems.
She seems so on top of her game. What's her story?"

"I know. She made the decision to be on the Recollections
side. I can't figure it out. I don't think she likes to interact with
too many of the residents."

Joan speaks her mind. Every time I see her, she looks irritable, wearing a constant expression of disdain on her face.

"Nobody likes being here," she tells me one day. "You just
deal with it."

The next time I visit, I stop by her nicely appointed
bedroom. She seems to spend most of her time here, away
from the other residents. It's like a fine hotel room complete
with a king-size bed and dark mahogany furniture.

Joan ushers me in as an aide is turning to go.

"Come on in. Have a seat. You know, they all think I'm
having a fling with him," she says, referring to the male aide
that just left.

"Really? Oh well, you know how people talk," I remark casually.

"Yeah, that's why I couldn't stand the other side," Joan retorts.

The conversation makes me think about "seasoned" people who believe younger people flirt with them. I hope I don't appear so foolish.

Vainly, I hope I still have a few more years of attracting lustful glances. I never did get women who detest men checking them out. I used to think, *Just you wait. One day they won't be looking.* My grandmother once said, "You know you're old when they don't look anymore."

After I collect my thoughts, I seek out the photographs adorning Joan's dresser. Her husband, fifteen or sixteen years her senior, is a classic handsome Italian. "Wow. He was a real looker," I say.

"Well, I thought so. He was a few years older and it worked out fine for me."

I notice the photos of her children. She has a son and a daughter. Joan remarks they'd better invite her over for Christmas. She tells me they overlooked her for Thanksgiving— neither sent her an invite.

I wonder if Joan actually does have dementia. Maybe Joan forgot that her son called and asked. Or maybe she went to her daughter's house on Thanksgiving Day and she can't remember.

Surely, a child wouldn't turn their back on a parent during the holidays. Would they?

If she were my mother, she'd be spending more than holidays with me. Even if Joan isn't the easiest person to live with, how hard can it be to spare the gift of time?

I know Joan is contentious. She has no patience for the other residents. Seeing a resident attempting to spit out a food particle into a tissue the other day, Joan turned away in disgust, muttering, "Jesus, Mary, and Joseph." Of course, it made me a little queasy too, but I elected not to telegraph it on my face.

Joan tells me she can't stand the "other side." "Too much stuff going on," she mutters with that familiar look of disdain. I've been on the other side. I suppose it could be overstimulating to someone who can't stand listening to other people's stories. Yet, the energy seems upbeat. The residents seem to like the socializing. It can't be all bad.

It must be that Joan doesn't like people. You know the type. These are the people who adore their pets and often prefer their company to the company of human beings. Sometimes I feel that way; just not often. I suspect Joan feels that way ninety-nine percent of the time.

As we finish our conversation, she says, "Come back again and see me some time."

I'm flattered to be invited into her lair. I must not be a "person" or at least not the kind of person Joan dislikes. Of course, I don't have drool hanging out of my mouth or suffer from uncontrollable outbursts. Hey, I'm fifty percent there as far as Joan is concerned.

Chapter 16

Holding His Hand

In the morning, after drinking my coffee, I heard the familiar ping of my phone notifying me of an incoming text message. It was from Joe.

Good morning. I have a lot to do today but I was wondering if you would like company when you go into Kirkland?

I grinned, feeling that spark of joy you get when someone surprises or delights you. I felt like I was eighteen years young. I thought it was interesting how he mentioned he had a lot to do—giving himself an out in case I replied that I didn't want company.

Me: *I would love that.*

Joe: *What time works for you?*

Me: *How about noon?*

Joe: *That works and we can grab some lunch. I can pick you up at your hotel if you want.*

Normally, I would never drive with someone I'd just met or hardly knew, just in case they were a serial killer. Since Joe didn't strike me as a serial killer and we had mutual friends, it seemed like a safe bet.

Me: *That would be great. See you soon.*

As I readied myself for our "date," if I could even call it

that, I started to wonder if this was such a good idea. After all, this was my boss's best friend! I kept having conflicting thoughts.

What's the big deal? You're meeting a friend.

What if it goes badly? Then what? How will I face Darren again? What will he think of me?

Remember that Joe lives in Seattle and I'm in California. There's not too much risk here.

The banter in my head went on and on until, suddenly, I decided: *I'm going and that's that.*

Joe picked me up about five minutes later than expected. Fashionably late I supposed. He was driving a large white suburban minivan. I thought, *Yeah, that's what a fixer-upper kind of manly man drives.*

He seemed a little nervous and maybe even a little sweaty. I started to look at him with fresh eyes. Was I physically attracted to this guy? I wasn't quite sure. I did like him a lot. Was I sexually attracted to him, though? That was always important to me, and I only dated men who met or exceeded my physical expectations.

When we arrived at downtown Kirkland, there was a street festival. Joe asked me if I would like to walk around. I agreed and, before I knew it, his massive hand had engulfed my tiny bony hand.

OH MY GAWD. He's holding my hand. What do I do? I don't know if I want him to hold my hand. Does this mean we're dating? OH MY GAWD. Get a grip, Jeanne. He's just holding your hand. What is the big deal? OH MY GAWD. This is my boss's best friend. I don't know that I should be doing this. Well, Jeanne, don't you think it's a bit LATE for that? Oh no, he's HOLDING MY HAND.

This rhetorical explosive confrontation with myself only

lasted about two minutes, though it felt like an eternity. Finally, I said to myself, *ENOUGH. Just hold his hand and enjoy his company. Be in the moment and just let it GO!*

When I finally gave myself permission to stop overanalyzing the situation and remain in the moment, it was remarkably relaxing. Again, it was as if I'd known Joe for much longer than forty-eight hours. As we strolled by the street fair vendors, he paused to ask me what I wanted to see.

WOW. He's actually interested in what I want to do. Is that possible?

We had lunch at Anthony's HomePort in Kirkland, sitting outside at a table overlooking Lake Washington. Joe said that growing up in Tampa, Florida, he loved being on the water. We had that in common. I'd always loved anything that involved water—swimming in it, sitting by it, walking near it. It was my Zen place.

We talked a lot about our lives, our marriages, our desires, and some of our hopes and dreams without disclosing too much personal information. He'd been married once for about ten years with no children and had nothing negative to say about his ex-wife. And still I didn't hear anything that threw up a red flag.

WAIT, there must be a red flag. There wasn't.

True to my pattern of self-sabotage, I began to look for other things I wouldn't like. *Is his nose too big? He has that ruddy complexion. Am I actually attracted to him?*

Yet, that smile.

Yes, Jeanne, focus on his smile and his eyes. Those eyes and that smile. Yes, very attractive.

OH MY GAWD. Really, Jeanne. Is that all you have? Stay in the moment. Enjoy his company. Can you try that for once? Why don't you do that. You might even enjoy his company.

After a number of interruptions from my rude self, I finally snapped back into the moment and started to listen to Joe. I'm not a great listener—it might be part of my personality, or there might be some biological component to blame. All I know is that my brain is always zipping around, making it very difficult for me to concentrate on conversations. I have to work hard to stay focused.

During our lunch, I learned that Joe was looking for a best friend, someone who would be a full partner. Someone to share experiences and dreams.

Wow. Is that romantic? What about lust? What about desire? What about pressing me against a wall and kissing me until I pass out?

Still, he was starting to grow on me. He was kind. He was a great listener. I wanted to know more.

When he dropped me off at my hotel, he gave me a quick hug and then left.

Okay. He's a gentleman. He keeps me guessing.

I'd had my share of slobbering fools and, gratefully, he wasn't one of those.

Could he be romantic, though? That question would have to wait for another date.

Chapter 17

The Email

On Monday, Joe texted me while he was at work.

Joe: *Enjoyed our time together and look forward to seeing you tomorrow.*

How sweet. Gotta love the follow-up. Follow-up is important. You want to know there's interest. You want to be sure it's not too much. I think men and women like the thrill of the chase. Most everyone likes a little bit of a challenge. At least I do.

Tuesday arrived and I was getting ready to drive to Darren's to have my ribeye supper and see Joe again. I changed into a flirty mint-green ruffled top and Capri pants. I felt fresh and a little bit sexy. I loved the anticipation.

When I arrived at the front door of Darren and Julie's home and knocked, Joe opened it within seconds. He took one look at me and said, "You look beautiful!"

He wrapped me in a warm embrace. Okay, suddenly I was hooked.

Growing up, I thrived on receiving compliments. I think that had to do with the way my mother sang my high praise. "You have it ALL," she would sing. "Looks, personality, smarts, and a sense of humor." Only years later did I realize there aren't too many mothers who build up their daughters with such confidence.

Some would say I received too much praise, that I suffer from an overinflated ego. I'm not so sure. My mother's praise was tempered by very direct criticism if I didn't act in the way she thought a young woman should behave. When I was seventeen, my boyfriend broke up with me a few weeks before Christmas. I was devastated and didn't want to come out of my room. My mother stormed down the hall, sounding like a wild animal on the hunt. She threw open the door and shouted, "Have some pride, for God's sake. You're going to get out of your room right now and help decorate the tree! And you're going to like it!"

She hated to see me cry. She hated to see me unhappy. I didn't understand this until I was a parent myself. This tough love response was her way of willing me into a change of emotion. While it didn't exactly help with the pain of the breakup, it did give me somewhere else to put my attention.

My mother adored me, doted on me, screamed at me, and once accused me of being a fool—the time she caught me in the sleeper sofa with the aforementioned boyfriend. Most of the time, she put me on the same pedestal where she'd placed my dad. I thought that pedestal was based on her desire to glorify my dad after his passing. I grew up thinking, *There's no way a man can make me feel like that.* That was before I met Joe.

During dinner that night, conversation with Joe flowed naturally. He laughed easily and that smile was really infectious. I could tell he liked me. He barely took his eyes off me, and he made me feel snug and warm in his presence.

Darren and Julie talked a lot about their friendship, their time at the cabin, and how much fun they had together. I was surprised that a single guy would have such a rich relationship with married people. They were more than friends; Joe was a like a brother to them.

At one point, Darren tried to show me a photo from Joe's yearly ritual of jumping into the Wenatchee River in early May when the water temperature hovers around 35 degrees. Like the people who take the polar bear plunge in the winter, this "tough" guy liked to push the limits.

Embarrassed, Joe shook his head, signaling to Darren that he wasn't ready for me to see him in a bathing suit. Fiercely protective, Julie exclaimed, "Darren, put that away. Joe doesn't want you showing that now."

Joe called an end to the evening around 9:30, explaining that his brother was in town and was staying at his house.

"Oh my goodness, you spent the evening here with me instead of being with your brother," I exclaimed.

Joe held his open palms out as if to weigh the situation. "Let's see," he said, "hang with brother Donny—or see Jeanne? Uh, I think I'll pick Jeanne."

That made me smile. His warmth and sweet humor filled my soul.

As we walked outside to our cars, I realized I was ready to kiss him if he made the move. I had a suspicion he might try it.

Touching my arm, Joe asked if he could come see me in California. He explained that one of his offices was in Long Beach, California, and he was often in town for business. I told him I would love that. He had a fishing trip planned for late August, and he promised to email me with details about a September visit.

He pulled me closer for an embrace. It felt so nice. I felt safe inside his strong arms.

Is he going to kiss me?

As if reading my mind, Joe pulled back and kissed me. It was soft and quick, as if we'd been friends for thirty years.

I wanted more. And yet, it left me very interested. I would have to wait a little while longer to get the kiss that would prove we had chemistry.

~

On August 15, 2014, I got an email from Joe. He was fishing on the Deshka River, somewhere in Alaska, a place I had no desire to visit.

This morning we woke at 3:30 a.m. and left by 4:00 a.m. to meet a boat at 6:00 a.m. to go fishing on the Little Susitna River. The trip started out in the rain. Later it cleared up and turned into a beautiful day. We got 5 silvers today and were off the river by noon. We came back to Steve's house and I passed out by 3:00. This has not been a relaxing vacation and I am exhausted. I can't wait to get home so I can relax. Have a wonderful weekend. Joe.

WHAT? What about me? Where was the commentary about how much he'd enjoyed meeting me and how much he was looking forward to seeing me again? No, this was just fish, fish, and more fish. I was perplexed. Maybe this fisherman wasn't going to be stimulating enough or complimentary enough to fit on that pedestal of mine.

I guess after he told me I looked beautiful the last time we were together, I expected him to gush a little. In time, I learned that Joe was a master of spacing out the "gush," making me fall hook, line, and sinker. No pun intended.

Joe contacted me when he returned, and we made arrangements to take a day trip to one of my favorite places, Catalina. He had a business trip planned in September, and we would spend the day together on Sunday. We planned to meet at his hotel and take the Catalina Express to the island for the afternoon.

Santa Catalina is just 22 miles from the Southern California coast. To me, it feels like an exotic island in the middle of nowhere. It offers wildlife, dive sites, breathtaking hikes, palm trees, and a beautiful art deco casino that serves as the focal point when you arrive into port.

When I learned that Joe had never toured Catalina, I was so excited to share the many adventures I'd had over the years exploring the island. When my son was little, he and I spent summer weekends there with my brother Russell and his family.

Russell and my cousin Hal captained the boat from Northern California and anchored it at Two Harbors. Jason and my sister-in-law, niece, and nephew spent hours jumping off the back of the boat, swimming in the blue waters, or taking the dinghy to shore.

I made several hikes with the kids, all the while worrying about my high-energy son falling off the edge of a cliff. He and my nephew, Ryan, scaled the rocks near shore, and I couldn't help but pray for their safe return when I saw them round a corner and disappear for what seemed like an eternity.

I was eager to return to the site of so many happy memories, and I didn't worry for a second about bringing Joe along. Born and raised in Tampa, Florida, Joe was a water boy. I knew he would enjoy the scenic day trip we'd planned together.

Chapter 18

The Test

I met Joe at his hotel and we drove to the port of Long Beach to take our sixty-minute trip to the island. I called him when I arrived a few minutes early. He wasn't quite ready and promised to be down in a few. When he rushed out to meet me, I noticed perspiration beading along his hairline. He kissed me lightly on the lips, and I could tell he was a little nervous.

As before, I started to question my attraction to him. *Am I doing the right thing? This is my BOSS'S BEST FRIEND. This could get very ugly. It could be a career-limiting move.*

I stopped my mental spiral and told myself to just try to have a good time. *Relax. He's a nice guy. Just enjoy the day.*

Yeah, right. No use telling this worrier to stop worrying.

When we stopped at the booth to purchase our tickets, I decided to test Joe's generosity. Money was a thing with me. I supported an ex-husband, including paying alimony. At this point in my life, I wanted a generous partner. I was looking for someone who wanted to spoil me rotten.

Don't get me wrong, I've never been a gold digger. I made a good living, and I didn't need a man for money. I simply didn't want to carry one on my back. Nor did I want to be the first one to pull out my wallet. A dear friend of mine once said, "You don't want to be a purse or a nurse."

My first test was to find out if Joe is *insistently* generous. My fantasy played out like this: I'd offer to pay for my boat ticket over. In protest, he would put his hand on my wallet and cast it aside and then smile and say, "I've got it covered." Happily, I'd defer. Voila! I'd know this was the man for me!

That was NOT how it played out. I approached the ticket counter and sweetly said, "How about if I pay for my ticket?" Without a moment's hesitation, Joe said "Okay" and waited for me to open my wallet.

WHAAAATTT? I immediately went into a tailspin ending in a long dark hallway where I suddenly felt trapped. This was not what I'd wanted to happen. He'd FAILED the test. This wasn't my dream man. He was like the others: selfish. Waiting to disappoint me at every turn.

I was consumed with negative thinking for what seemed like hours. I was trying to rationalize his decision to allow me to pay. Well, I had offered to pay. After all, we were living in a different world now, even though I was from a generation that expected the man would pay for just about everything, at least in the early stages of the dating game.

It was hard to get out of my head that day. I was about ready to give up on Joe being the one. It's not that I was ready to consider a long-term marriage proposal; I just always had that "MAYBE he could be the one" in the back of my mind. *Maybe this time someone will surprise me. Maybe this time someone will put me on that pedestal my mother always described. Maybe this time there really is a knight in shining armor.*

It suddenly dawned on me that if I wanted to get through six hours on the magical island of Catalina, I needed to move past this. I decided to give Joe the benefit of the doubt. Perhaps he was just trying to be polite and felt he would offend me if he offered to pay, knowing I was independent and capable of paying for myself.

So after two hours of waffling between devil Jeanne and angel Jeanne, angel Jeanne took control and decided she would give Joe another shot.

I would not open up my wallet for anything else and see how it played out. Joe graciously paid for lunch and a cocktail or two during our time together. So I decide it was all okay now. He could stay.

Once I got over my insane thinking, and my hypersensitivity to the money card, I fully enjoyed our date. Somehow this man brought out a calmness in me I'd never felt before.

Strolling by the dark-blue waters of the Pacific Ocean, overlooking the stunning cliffs that showcase pine forests and chamise chaparral vegetation, he held my hand and we talked about our passion for water. He stopped to take in some of the architectural elements of the Catalina Casino, making comments about the structure of the silver-and-gold-accented concrete columns and trying to figure out how it was built.

I found his interest in structures incredibly sexy and masculine. Suddenly, I felt a stronger attraction to this "maintenance man" named Joe. *He can build stuff.*

And then came the next test of any relationship—physical chemistry. Physical chemistry can be tricky. You can be so infatuated with lust that you lose all sense of perspective about your emotional chemistry.

That said, attraction is attraction and you have to start somewhere. When Joe kissed me that afternoon, it wasn't the brotherly kiss I received at Darren's house. This was a full-on lustful, romantic kiss that sent the butterflies fluttering madly in my stomach. Standing there in Joe's arms overlooking the exquisite ocean with the hot sun at my back, I was on top of the world.

This was the kiss that said, *WOW. Maybe this is the ONE after all.*

Joan Again

Joan loves birds and puzzles. For Christmas, I wrap a beautiful jigsaw puzzle for Joan and hand it to her, suppressing a grin.

"For me?" she exclaims.

"Yes, I know how much you love presents. I just had to get this for you."

I'm humbled by her gracious expression and excitement over this small gift.

When she opens it and discovers the puzzle, the look on her face says I've handed her the keys to the magic kingdom. Her aging fingers trace the outline of the blue-and-orange birds. "This is the most WONDERFUL gift I've ever gotten. I love these birds. Look how magnificent they are!"

My throat constricts and I have to hold back tears. Her extravagant emotion humbles me.

"This is the nicest thing anyone has ever done for me."

Oh, Joan, really? It can't be. This must be the dementia. Is this a bad thing or a good thing? How sad that she can't recall other more meaningful gifts. Maybe it's good that in this time and space, Joan believes this to be such an extraordinary gift.

"I'm glad." I force a smile. "I wanted to do this for you because I know how much you love birds."

"Oh, I do," Joan oozes. "They are my favorite. I can't thank you enough for doing this for me."

As the weeks pass, Joan's illness takes its toll, and her puzzle becomes another lost memory. She keeps asking about her daughter. An aide explains that her daughter has brain cancer. They don't want to tell Joan the news, so Joan just wonders why her daughter doesn't come see her.

Heartbreaking. Heart-wrenching. I tell her that I'm sure her daughter will visit soon. What else can I say? Is it better for her to know the sad truth or just think her daughter doesn't care? There's no winning this battle.

When Joan passes not long after, I'm grieved by her death. I've lost another friend. Will we meet again in heaven? I hope so. I'll be sure to bring a bird puzzle with me.

Chapter 19

There's Something about Joe

I couldn't shake the feeling that my mother had picked Joe for me. Not only did I discover my mother and Joe shared a birthday, May 23, I could no longer deny that he had the "pedestal effect." Every quality my mom described in my father—strong, protective, full of integrity, passionate, demonstrative, loyal, and supportive—revealed itself in Joe.

First of all, he never disappointed me. Every time he promised something, he delivered. From the long-distance plans to the monthly flower delivery, I could count on Joe to be consistent.

This relationship was different. It was romantic, exciting, intense, provocative, engaging, lustful, and there wasn't an ounce of drama to it. WHAT? I was the queen of drama. I acted it, attracted it, encouraged it, and had sought it in almost every romantic encounter I'd ever had. The question was why?

Despite all the excitement of this new relationship, there was a stillness, a calmness, a comfortable quality that made it seem almost too easy. The first evening Joe visited my home in California, he said, "Is this weird? Wait a minute, forget it."

"No," I insisted, "tell me what you're thinking."

"I don't know. It just seems comfortable, you and me,

doesn't it?" he said shyly. "It feels so nice, like we've known each other for a while."

"Yes, it does. It's really nice."

I was learning to live in the moment. I let the relationship thrive. For the first time, I didn't sabotage it. Though I'm certain I came close a few times.

Joe told me he'd actually sabotaged a number of relationships too. When we're not ready to commit, we pick people we know will never work out. And then we get disappointed or, worse, hurt in the end.

There was something about Joe. It was that calmness. It was his quiet delivery. It was that winning smile that won him a lot of friends and no enemies. Everyone wanted to be around that energy. And I was no exception.

Chapter 20

Long-Distance Romance

After Catalina, Joe and I began our long-distance relationship, which consisted of me flying out for business trips every other month or so. In between, he would fly to California for a business trip or just book a weekend to spend time with me at my home in Simi Valley.

By then my son, Jason, was nineteen years old and far from the defiant fourteen-year-old who once threatened to knife any man who dared come into our home. Though that may sound alarming and a bit cray cray, I knew it came from the mouth of an immature young boy who was highly possessive of his mother.

Still, I wondered if he would accept Joe, and I carried young Jason's voice in the back of my mind.

One day after I told him about Joe, Jason said, "Mom, I don't care if you date."

I shouldn't have been surprised; the attitude seemed fitting for him at that age. He didn't care much about anything unless it was a hot girl or a fabulous video game. He was self-absorbed and slightly defiant, though still impressionable.

Once they met, Joe and Jason hit it off, eventually becoming good friends. Joe grew to love my son and played a very important role in his developing manhood. A great role model, Joe is a black belt and a sensei, a teacher of Okinawan martial arts. In his spare time, he taught several young people in his dojo (his garage), training them to compete at various karate competitions.

In the karate world, respect is a big deal. It signifies the respect for the knowledge, skills, and rank of the trainer and honors those who teach. A parent of two of Joe's former students told me that when she asked her kids to tidy up, her pleas fell on deaf ears. Yet the minute she informed Joe of her predicament, he would set them down and have a come-to-Jesus meeting of the minds. To the parents' delight, the boys completed all their chores after that and continued to do so. When Joe was not pleased, it was not good, they said. The boys were more afraid of Joe than they were of their parents. They weren't afraid of retribution; they were afraid of disappointing Joe.

Joe commanded respect. He had a quiet sense of discipline and a straightforward way of saying exactly what he expected without attacking, demeaning, or intimidating. In time I grew to have a healthy respect for him and that made our relationship all the more solid.

Meanwhile, we continued to see one another for two or three days every month, and eventually that meant me staying at his home in Redmond while I commuted to the office in Bellevue.

I loved playing house. One of my favorite things was to get up in the morning and make Joe a nice breakfast while I watched through the kitchen window as he worked in his massive yard, pulling weeds, raking leaves, and mowing the lawn. I considered anything larger than a postage-stamp-sized yard, which was the norm in California, to be very large indeed.

About a third of an acre, the yard was his baby. The former owners had created a Zen-like garden complete with diverse flowers, plants, trees, fragrant blossoms, and a wide range of textures. When one plant went dormant, another would bloom like a powerful fireworks show ebbing and flowing all year long. Joe tended to every nook and cranny of the yard, and I loved watching him in his playground.

It seemed like we were, dare I say, married. For the first time since my initial separation more than eight years ago, I started to think about marriage.

Despite our closeness, it seemed like a lifetime before I heard Joe say the words "I love you." It was actually about six months from the day we met at the Chateau. It became a little bit of a sticking point for me. My girlfriends would say that all of Joe's actions illustrated that he was in love. He called me practically every night, sent me flowers every month, and was always making plans for another visit. There was also a lot of "nesting" going on, and we talked often about future plans.

One trip in particular was very telling. We were having dinner at Darren and Julie's home along with a few other friends. At one point, Joe came up behind me and flirtatiously pinched my behind. No one knew but us. Later, I told him how much I enjoyed his secret display of affection.

He said, "Well, actually, I'm hoping to do that for thirty more years."

I couldn't believe my ears! *What? He hasn't told me he loves me, yet he's talking about thirty years together.* I held on to that comment, replaying it again and again in my head. It made me *feel* loved. It made me feel that Joe saw we had something special.

Mrs. Calabria

Mrs. Calabria is a well-loved human being. The aides tell me she spent thirty-three years as an elementary school teacher and that some of her former students still keep in touch with her. Teaching is her crowning glory. I walk up to her wheelchair, stoop down, and greet her at eye level.

"Hi there, Mrs. Calabria. How are you today?"

I ask her to tell me about her teaching.

"I loved every minute of it. I gave to them. They gave to me," she says, pointing her index finger to her heart. "One day, there were hundreds of them. They were running to me. It was unbelievable. I knew every one of them. I knew them all. They were running to me." Tears stream down her cheeks and her eyes glimmer with happiness.

I hold back my own tears. She repeats herself and her words aren't always clear, yet I believe I understand. I think she must be remembering a time when she returned to the school after a prolonged absence. Perhaps it was after she retired. Or perhaps she was returning after a long summer. Whatever the case, her students were thrilled to see her.

This is the teacher you never forget. This is the teacher who is mother, coach, leader, disciplinarian, and friend all rolled into one. It's the teacher whose name we always recall. It's the teacher we would like to see again before we leave this earth. What a remarkable human being. I'm both saddened and touched by her story.

"How wonderful that you loved what you did for a living, Mrs. Calabria. So many people spend their entire life without that kind of fulfillment. And you made such a difference."

"Yes, I wish I was still there," she cries.

I wish I could take her there now. I would whisk her away in a time machine and watch her magic come alive. I can almost hear her: "Claudia, you mustn't forget to do your homework, darling. Homework is very important, and I know you will do the right thing."

This is how I imagine the young Mrs. Calabria. Caring, loving, and forgiving.

On another day, I find Mrs. Calabria sitting alone in the parlor.

"Come here, come here," she hastens me over.

"Hello, Mrs. Calabria. How are you?"

"Where am I?" she asks.

"You're home, dear. You're safe here."

"They're making me feel not like me. I don't feel like me. What are they doing to me?" She grabs my arm in fear and protest.

I don't know what to say. She is confused, most likely due to the dementia or possibly the medication. What can I say to comfort her? I grasp for the right words.

I reach for her hand. "Mrs. Calabria, I know you are confused, and I'm sorry. This is a nice place and you have to trust me that the people here are taking good care of you. I know it's hard, Mrs. Calabria. You are okay. I promise you are okay."

The words seem inadequate for this heroic figure. How many future leaders did she shape in her lifetime? I imagine one student becomes a peacemaker saving nations from disaster. One is a masterful artist because Mrs. Calabria said he had talent. One is an artful parent raising a child who becomes a doctor and saves the lives of cancer patients.

The hundreds of running children become thousands. These thousand souls go on to start a career, begin a family, save a heart, save a soul, save a life. It started with a teacher named Mrs. Calabria.

I stroke her hand one more time and ask her to tell me about her teaching. She smiles and begins again.

Chapter 21

Love Language

Before he met Joe, my brother Russell insisted that I read a book called *The Five Love Languages*. Written in 1995 by Gary Chapman, the book details the five ways that people feel loved and appreciated. They are: words of affirmation, acts of service, receiving gifts, quality time, and physical touch.

The notion is that we all have a primary love language—one of the five types is our dominant love language. Understanding these differences and learning to speak your partner's primary language is the key to a happy relationship.

Honestly, I'm such an attention seeker, I think I have all five languages. I want it all!

After Joe and Russell finally met, my brother and I had dinner together. He was intent on talking about Joe. Fear struck me like a lightning bolt. *Is he going to tell me something bad about Joe?*

Russell said, "I want to tell you about Joe. You've got a GREAT guy. I mean, this guy is beyond great. He's an incredible guy."

Whew. I liked where this was going.

"The thing is, Jeanne, you have a thing about needing validation." He emphasized the word *validation* as if it were a four-letter word. The fear was back. *Uh-oh.*

He went on, "You need affirmation. You need everyone to compliment you, to tell you how wonderful you are, to tell you all these things."

What's your point?

"Whereas Joe, he shows love through action. He shows his love in the things that he does. That is his love language. What I'm telling you is, don't SCREW it up."

Suddenly, I pictured my mother right next to Russell, cigarette in hand, vehemently nodding in agreement. "Jeanne, he's absolutely right. Don't RUIN it."

Okay, loud and clear. Still, I couldn't help wanting the words of affirmation, and the physical touch, and the acts, and the gifts.

So, despite the admonitions from my brother and my deceased mother, who occasionally makes an appearance in my mind, I still wasn't quite satisfied without hearing "I love you" from Joe.

Joe later told me he muttered "I love you" after only three months of dating, as he was leaving the hotel room where we stayed during a business trip in California. I don't recall hearing it. At the time, he was absolutely horrified that it had slipped off his tongue. *Holy crap, what did I just say?* he thought to himself.

In December of that same year, he said the words again. This time in a playful way after teasing me about something I said.

That didn't count in the Jeanne Corvese playbook of romance. I wanted him to gaze longingly into my eyes and say it very slowly, "Darling, I want you to know that I'm madly in love with you, and I want to spend the rest of my life with you and with your two cute dogs." Well, maybe I'm exaggerating a little bit. Yet I hadn't gotten the sincere declaration of love I was hoping to receive.

I wanted to be careful to let Joe be the man, giving him the time he needed while finding a way to encourage the words. I knew he loved me. He was highly affectionate, attentive, and always looking for ways to please me.

For Christmas, he gave me the key to his house. It wasn't just any key—it was a key engraved with leopard print. Anyone who knows me knows I love animal print and bling. He knew it too. One friend said, "Wow, he really gets you."

Going back to *The Five Love Languages*, I needed words of affirmation. And those words were a big deal to Joe. After Christmas, I said to him on more than one occasion, "It's important for me to know how you feel about me."

I hated that I had to ask. It felt like it was forced. It felt like coercion. Well, okay, I guess it was.

So I waited and waited and waited. I waited until about six months into our relationship. Then came Valentine's Day. I was in town on business and staying at Joe's house in Redmond. Joe picked out several sweet cards for me. None of them were signed "Love." Instead, Joe had written "XO" at the close. That morning, he prepared his famous frittata breakfast and decorated the table with flowers.

It was the COMPLETE romantic display of affection. I mentioned I needed more. I remember feeling somewhat resentful that I even had to ask. I didn't understand why it was so difficult for him to say it.

We were listening to the Basia station on Pandora and a beautiful ballad by Matt Bianco called "Say the Words" came on. The lyrics speak to a lover who never gets to hear the words they long for. I could relate.

Could he say the words? Would he say the words? The lyrics continued to haunt me.

Earlier in our courtship, when I was lying in Joe's strong arms one day, I said, "You make me happy." SILENCE. I waited for what felt like an eternity for him to respond.

"Well…" I said, "do I make you happy?"

He rolled over and very directly told me, "I don't say things just because someone says it to me."

Oh. Wow.

I snapped, "I'm so sorry that's so DIFFICULT for you to say." I rolled over and out of his arms, feeling hurt and rejected. I didn't understand why it was so difficult for him to reciprocate.

We went a few rounds on that one, and I'm certain he reassured me that he had feelings for me. I worried that I was pushing him away. Yet, I felt my request wasn't over the top. It wasn't like I was asking him to marry me and have my children and adopt the dogs too.

I later learned that when Joe says something, he means it.

Back to Valentine's Day 2015. I finished my wonderful breakfast and went upstairs to shower. While I was finishing up, Joe came upstairs, flung open the shower door, and said, "I do love you" and kissed me quickly on the lips. He disappeared before I could answer.

I stood frozen in the shower not believing what I'd just heard. It was typical Joe. He got me off guard. He got me hook, line, and sinker.

Beautiful Legs

I will not retire while I've still got my legs and my makeup box.
—Bette Davis

One day Miriam gives us all a shock when she struts proudly into the room wearing only a shirt and an adult diaper. Her legs are strong yet wrinkly as an elephant's legs. A few of the residents appear disgusted. Nancy mouths, "Oh dear Lord." I am speechless.

One of the aides reacts quickly, suppressing the urge to laugh. "Miriam, my dear, where are your pants?"

Miriam responds matter-of-factly. "They are in my room."

"Well, my dear, we must get them back on," the aide says, attempting to shuffle Miriam along.

Determined to leave the room with a shred of dignity, Miriam looks directly at me and says, "My mom always said I had beautiful legs."

I laugh out loud. "Yes, you do have outstanding legs, my dear."

On my way out, I make a point to stop by Miriam's room. I want to check out those young, beautiful legs.

I spot a black-and-white photograph of her lying outstretched on a rock, wearing a white linen shirt and a pair of mid-length shorts. She's propped up on her arms, her legs bent toward her chest. The image portrays a woman who is half sex-kitten and half intellectual Girl Scout.

With that broad smile, Miriam is as sure and steady as the rock she's perched upon. She looks at the camera with a knowing glance that seems to say, "Go on. Make my day."

As if watching the scene unfold in real time, I imagine her mom asking her to pose, "Hey, Miriam, let's show off those gorgeous gams."

I'm so glad Miriam remembers she has gorgeous legs.

Chapter 22

Whoever Said "Never Say Never" Was Right

Things between me and Joe progressed quickly once the four-letter word was uttered. Having heard him declare his love, I felt complete. It was the affirmation I needed to know we were working toward something; I didn't have to wonder what the future would bring.

We talked more openly about the future and the possibilities. One day after we had breakfast together, I mentioned that people at work were speculating about when I would move to Seattle or even get married. OOPS, it had popped out. I guess I just couldn't resist testing the waters.

Joe smiled and said, "Yeah, I'm sure they're wondering about that."

I responded by saying, "Well, I guess since my job is here and your job is here, it would ultimately make more sense to have me move here."

"Yes, that would be logical."

Wow. Did I just say I might move to Seattle? The city of rain. Not to mention seasonal depression.

After living in Southern California for more than thirty

years in a perpetual state of sunshine euphoria, strangely enough, I found Seattle strikingly beautiful even when it rained. Surrounded by water and covered in lush evergreens, the city was an incredible landscape for any artist. Yet could I live here? And for how long? Forever? Ten years?

Suddenly, I was picturing myself moving in with Joe, looking out the kitchen window and watching him work, waking up every morning with his arms around me, receiving flowers every week, and sleeping beside him and two dachshunds every night!

I actually liked the idea. Then the record scratched loudly. My twenty-year-old son was not independent. How could I leave him? My only child, my baby, my heart—he was everything to me. Leaving him would be impossible.

I wanted Joe to know it could take years before I could move to Seattle to live with him. Would he wait all that time? Could we sustain a long-distance relationship for that long?

There is no way I'll be ready to move soon. My son would have to become independent. Right now he can barely hold down a job. His father was in Florida and offered no help in supporting Jason.

"Joe, it could be five years before I'm ready to make that kind of move. Jason is not ready to move out, and I'd have to be sure he would be okay if I left him. Could you really wait that long?"

His answer almost knocked me out of my seat. "You never know. You could be moving next year."

Hello, Shirley? Did you hear that? It was as if she whispered in my ear, "Jeanne, you never know what's around the corner."

As it turned out, Joe was right. Circumstances changed in ways I never could have imagined. That conversation happened on February 14, 2015. By April of 2016, I was moving in with Joe—one year and two months later. Never say never.

Chapter 23

Music and the Brain

Music is probably the greatest gift to mankind. It boosts creativity and helps us relax. It increases our focus, heals our worries, and eases our loneliness.

When I was growing up, music was a constant in my home. Every holiday, jazz musicians gathered in our home, crowding around my mother as she played and sang her heart out. She would goad me to stand up on a chair and sing show tunes to the small crowd gathered in our living room. Occasionally, she would even play stripper music and have me shake my butt to the tune.

I was a real hit back in the seventies. Everyone in attendance would chuckle with amusement that such a small child could command the audience. The laughter encouraged me to ham it up. The more they laughed, the more I wanted to be the center of attention. This remains a part of my personality to this day.

Music has an incredible way of engaging our memory mechanisms. I've seen this time and again during my visits with seniors. Even my seniors with dementia in the most catatonic of states react to music—they often sing along with the lyrics. It fascinates me.

I love to see my seniors come alive when the music starts. I think it takes them back to a more youthful time; a time when life was full of hope, promise, and dreams yet to be fulfilled. When you walk into a senior home, sometimes you'll hear music playing from a different era. It has a way of transporting you to another time and space.

Today, whenever I hear the standards of Sinatra, Peggy Lee, Nat King Cole, or Mel Tormé, I'm that little girl again, sharing the piano stool with my mom. She is looking at me lovingly, moving her slim, tiny fingers over the keyboard, singing in her smoky voice.

Whenever I had friends over, I couldn't wait to show them what my mom could do. "Mommy, please play some ragtime for my friend Darla, pretty please." She protested, "Jeanne, ragtime is not my thing. It's a difficult thing to play."

I insisted until she finally sat down and began to lean into the required syncopation while handling the octaves. When you're playing ragtime, you play the first person's part with your left hand and the second person's part with your right hand. Since I can't walk and chew gum at the same time, I can see why it would be challenging.

I was her greatest fan. And she was my greatest fan. Looking back, I feel sad that I didn't get to spend more time with my mother. Somehow, though, when the music comes on, especially when it's a song my mom played frequently, I feel her in the room. I feel her in my heart. I feel her in more powerful ways than words can describe.

Chapter 24

The Universe Says It's Time

When I returned to California from that February Seattle trip with Joe, things changed in ways I hadn't foreseen, in ways that prepared me for my future move. A kitchen pipe burst and saturated my flooring and perimeter walls.

I contacted a water damage remediation company to assess the damage and identify action steps. They determined that my entire kitchen needed to be replaced and my insurance company would pay for it. Great news, right? I did want a new kitchen, and it would add substantial value to my home.

What I didn't know was that it would be a very long, drawn out, and painful process. When it was all said and done, I was without a kitchen for seven long months. That meant setting up kitchen camp in my dining room, washing dishes in the bathroom, and having my kitchen area sealed off with a sea of plastic that made me feel like I was living in a bubble.

It was just a bit inconvenient—it certainly wasn't the end of the world. Joe reminded me that I was getting a new kitchen out of it. That was the most important thing. The hard part was chasing down the contractors and having to review a list of fixes that were completely out of my comfort zone. Joe walked me through every step of the process. It was hard to discuss it remotely because Joe insisted on explaining every nauseating mechanical detail so I could better instruct the insurance company and contractors.

I hated it. I wanted no part of sifting through details such as batt insulation, mortar beds, and V-caps for edging and corners. I can barely find my way out of a shopping mall—how was I to understand the complexities of rebuilding a kitchen?

Joe patiently tried to guide me through it only to have me erupt in frustration, which he perceived as anger toward him. He would threaten to extricate himself from helping me if I continued to behave so impatiently. I didn't blame him.

Somehow, Joe and I got through it and in September of 2015, I had a brand-new kitchen, complete with hardwood engineered flooring. During that year, my son's father moved back to Simi Valley, and Jason decided it was time to move in with him.

WAIT JUST ONE MINUTE. Jason is moving out? Okay, that's good, right? Now I can plan my move to live with Joe. I was already preparing Jason that I wanted to "one day" move to Seattle and live with Joe. I'd encouraged him to figure out how he would live independently.

Suddenly, I was torn between feeling great about having the freedom to live out my second act and this incredible sense of grief that I was losing my baby boy. Sobbing in an Albertson's parking lot, I called Joe.

"He's moving in with his dad," I cried.

"That's great, honey. Now you don't have to worry about leaving him," Joe said.

"Then why do I feel so sad?" I wailed. "I know that it's good for me, I just feel so depressed about it. I feel so lost."

"Do you still want to be with me?" Joe asked with a hint of insecurity.

"Of course I do, honey. I've never been more sure of anything in my life. This is separate. This is just me having to deal with the emotions of actually leaving Jason instead of him moving away from me. I will somehow get through it. Right now, I'm just so sad about it."

I hung up from that call and cried in the parking lot for another half hour. I can still feel that emotion. It's one thing for a son to pack up and leave his mother. It's another thing for a mother to pack up and leave her son. It's not the natural order of events.

I felt selfish, and mothers shouldn't be selfish. It was time to call in the professionals. I called Jake, a therapist I consulted periodically. "Jake, I feel so guilty about leaving Jason."

"What's your worst fear?" he asked me.

"That I'm leaving Jason with his dad, an inferior parent. I'm the better parent. I know what's best for him and now I'm leaving him with his dad," I cried emphatically.

"Let's get this straight. You're the *better* parent. Jason is old enough to navigate around any issues that may crop up. He has a healthy sense of selfishness. In fact, your leaving will help Jason figure it all out on his own. You have this tendency to try and rescue Jason. That's not what he needs. You won't be able to rescue him when you're farther away. You can still be there for him in the same way you are today. I think that will be very good for both of you."

I knew Jake was right. After that I felt somewhat better. I was finally able to begin preparing for my second chapter.

Chapter 25

The Move

I was ready—or ready as I'd ever be. By late March of 2016 I was packed and loaded, set to leave my only son, who was my world, and the town I'd lived in for the last thirty years. Many of the seniors I'd visited had passed away, and I said my goodbyes to the aides I'd befriended. I decided to rent out my house in the highly unlikely event that things didn't work out with Joe.

Emotionally speaking, I wasn't ready to leave everything behind in my life. Somehow, holding on to the one thing I worked so hard to get (my home) made me feel I wasn't walking away from everything.

Sadness and a myriad of fears got the best of me. The movers came early and were asking me a million and one questions. Unable to concentrate on more than one thing at a time, I was all over the map—confused, overwhelmed, and mentally exhausted.

I'd start something in the kitchen and a mover would ask me a question, so I'd leave what I was doing and forget what was happening in the kitchen. Repeatedly, Joe had to bring me back to the task at hand. Today, whenever I have trouble focusing, Joe will say to me, "Jeanne, we're in the kitchen now.

Focus." It's become a mantra in our relationship.

The cleaning crew asked me to go through each room to make sure everything was in order. I walked into my son's room first. All the memories of our years there suddenly floated up in front of me. The two of us playing on the floor with his baseball cards. Jason lighting up with joy when I put his very own Christmas tree in his room. Jason lying in bed with Tasha Bear, our sweet Doxie-mix puppy whom he'd insisted we get when he was twelve years old.

Walking from room to room, I convulsed with sobs. I remembered holidays, friends, first puppy steps up the staircase, warm toasty fires, dates that went sideways, children putting on plays in the garage. I saw the tape marks on the garage door that a young Jason put up that read, "STRIKE." He'd throw a softball against the door and wanted to frame it just so. Sobs poured out of me, exploding with a such a fierce wail that I could not contain them. Joe held my hand quietly and let me get it all out. And boy did I get it all out.

I felt a visceral reaction to the pain and joy represented in every room. Looking over the staircase down into the living room, I remembered the time I asked my ex-husband to leave, not knowing it would be for good. Sadness and guilt flooded my being. The house had ghosts and the ghosts were still there. I was relieved to be walking away from the spirits that had cohabited with me all these years. Good riddance, I thought. Now I can start fresh. Isn't that a good thing?

It hurt so much I thought I was going to die. I felt Joe's powerful stillness, his silent strength and love. It engulfed me with courage, warmth, and calmness even through the emotions that overtook my soul.

Then Jason showed up to say goodbye. Suddenly, leaving

the house didn't seem like the hardest part of the move. The knife went into my stomach with a force I can't describe. "Mom, it's okay, I'm fine," he said. He joked that he was going to miss the dogs most of all.

We laughed. "I'll be okay. I'll be okay." It was time to go. I wished with every cell in my body that I could be in two places at the same time. I wished I could move in with Joe *and* stay here and be with Jason.

I followed Joe outside and buckled up for the journey forward.

~

The dogs and I were loaded in the car and on our way to Redmond, Washington, our new home. I told Joe that Tasha Bear, my oldest dog, would be nervous driving for that long and would need tranquilizers. Joe suggested we try it without drugging her, saying it might be better if I were tranquilized. I laughed and we tried it his way.

Both dogs proved me a liar. They were as calm as can be and enjoyed an occasional stop along the way. I think it was due to Joe's calm energy—to this day they are completely different dogs. Tasha Bear is no longer neurotic, and Oscar insists that Joe is his person, following his every move around the house. I try to tell them that it was I who adopted them from a horrid existence.

I also insisted that the dogs would not pee or poo in the rain, so we'd have to figure out a way to protect them and allow them to go comfortably. Joe looked at me the way a parent looks at a child who is making up a story and said, "We'll see."

As it turned out, the dogs learned to poo and pee in the rain. And I learned how to wear a hood, instead of using an umbrella, which is the custom in Seattle.

The trip took us about two days with a one-night stay at an inn along the way. We arrived at Joe's Redmond home around midnight and began our new relationship as a live-together couple. Before the move, Joe and I talked about marriage. We agreed that marriage was in the cards for us; it was just a matter of time.

I of course had a different version of "time." I expected to be engaged within a few months of moving in. After all, I'd made the ultimate sacrifice and left everything and everyone I'd known, including my twenty-year-old son.

Joe knew how I felt about waiting and quietly reminded me that I would have to let him be a man; I needed to wait for the actual date. He assured me he had a date and time in place for this momentous event.

This was difficult for me to do because it meant letting go and letting love do its thing. As an adult child of an alcoholic mother, I'd struggled with control my entire life. Ask any of my past loves. I was the MAN in my life.

With Joe, I didn't need to be the man, and it was a breath of fresh air. I could trust what he said and what he did. I knew that he always put me first. No one in my life had ever put me first.

I tell young women today, if you want to know if you're with the right man, you have to trust your gut instinct. If you have a burning, gnawing feeling in your stomach, the kind you get when you see red flags, listen to it. It's *always* right.

Never once in our relationship did I have that gnawing feeling. Was I unsure and nervous about our future together? You bet. Did I believe in my heart that he'd come through for me? Hell yeah!

And he did. Joe came through for me with flying colors.

Chapter 26

Love Letters

While looking for material for my book, I started with a box of letters my father wrote to my mother when they were about to be married. There were two letters missing that I remembered him writing. One was a letter describing how she captivated a room. The other was written in anger when she couldn't decide between him and another man she loved. You may remember that my mother was perfectly capable of loving two men at the same time!

These letters are my sacred connection to the father I lost when I was nine years old. Written when my dad was thirty, they say a lot to me about his character, his passions, his dreams, and his steadfast adoration for my mother, Shirley. He even wrote her a letter before he died and hid it away for her to read after his passing. It was a haunting prediction that he wasn't long for this world.

To my delight, I found both letters in a box of miscellaneous cards and mementos I'd tucked away when Joe and I moved into our home.

The best part of rereading this letter was noting the date. It was written April 16, 1956, a few years before my birth, to the date. Reading between the lines, it would appear that he and my mother played music together at the Stuyvesant Hotel in Buffalo, New York, on a Tuesday evening. He played sax and she played piano.

Dear Shirley,

Gwen remarked how lovely you looked Tuesday night. Naturally, everyone in the place was digging you and I felt as proud as a peacock. I must say you did something for the Stuyvesant room. You projected life in its fullest meaning. You couldn't understand why everyone was coming over to you, but I did. I study people wherever I play, and the reason why this room is morbid is that the people that come here are about all the same. They're all trying to express themselves (the reason for the noisiness) as to enjoyment. They're mostly businesspeople, salesmen, etc. rather lonely and so wrapped up in their small world that someone as outstanding as you reflecting the true brilliance of down-to-earth beauty shocks them to an extent that they would enjoy just being in your company. Shirley, you're the type who projects happiness, loveliness, and warmth, which so many people lack and try so hard to attain and ultimately when they see they cannot capture it, just being near someone who has these qualities is satisfaction in itself...anyone who can be in your presence and not be happy would be a moron or self-possessed—one or the other.

Well, I think this manuscript is about completed. It was just a short note to try and relate how much I love you and miss you—"I need your love so badly." Now take care of yourself and keep laughing, honey. I'll see you shortly.

All my love,
Dick

My mother said I should find a man like my father, one who puts me on a pedestal. Over the years, though, I was lucky if I found a date who could let me finish a sentence. Where in the hell would I find the man and this pedestal he's supposed to put me on?

It was such a romantic time, a different time, a time where gush was pouring out of the woodwork. I grew up on that gush. I grew up thinking I would find it.

And then I GREW up. I gave up thinking I would find a person who could make me feel like a princess. It was a fairy tale. It was like Santa Claus, a fable that builds us up only to disappoint us in the end.

Sitting there on the floor of Joe's house, the house we would now share together, all I could think was, *Thank goodness Shirley was determined to prove me wrong.*

Chapter 27

The Engagement

Months went by and I waited for that moment—not exactly patiently. It didn't come in the summer. It didn't come in the fall. By winter of 2016, I wondered if Christmas would bring the "special moment." Joe made sure to tell me that I would not get a ring on Christmas.

I took that statement figuratively as in "there will be no ring during the holidays." In hindsight, I see that in order to throw me off, he meant the statement in the *literal* sense. I would not get engaged on Christmas Day.

For Christmas Eve, Joe made plans to take me to the home of his friends the Radcliffes. They were part of a very social club of friends that Joe had collected throughout the years. Like all of Joe's friends, the Radcliffes were amazing people—kind, funny, nonjudgmental, and full of joy.

Every Christmas Eve, the Radcliffes hosted Christmas Eve for about thirty of their friends in their exquisite, spacious Seattle home. The menu included everything from Alaskan crab legs to catered soups and roasted sirloin. It was a magnificent spread suited for kings. This year was no exception, and their group had grown larger, which meant putting up a heated tent outside where everyone could sit, eat, and socialize.

It was my first time having the Radcliffe Christmas Eve experience. When I walked through the door with Joe, the place was loud and bustling with energy. The friends and their grown children were milling about, drinking lots of wine, and maneuvering in and out of the kitchen, the heated tent, and the family room.

Unable to get a word in edgewise, I meandered through the house, admiring the low lighting and candles. My mother always said to turn the lights down during a party so guests would stay longer. Not to mention that low lighting is very flattering. She created a nightclub-like experience, which I still do to this day whenever I host a party.

I briefly wondered if Joe was really throwing me off and planning to ask me to marry him in front of all his friends. I quickly discounted the thought after trying to digest the many conversations happening simultaneously.

I've always had difficulty immersing myself in big crowds. Easily overwhelmed and overstimulated in larger gatherings, I find it hard to concentrate on one thing. It probably goes back to my childhood; I always felt I was missing out unless I was the center of attention.

So here I was with a very large crowd and not too many ways to *be* the center of attention. That was okay because I had enough pleasure just dangling on the arm of my handsome man and looking forward to the evening's festivities, highly entertaining in their own right.

The Radcliffes had a close friend named Evan, a very successful business professional and company president … and an infamous prankster. Described to me as a "shock jock," he was someone who went to great lengths to stun ordinary everyday people.

Friends told me about a time when they were out dining at a very posh restaurant, and Evan took a $300 bottle of wine and smashed it on the floor. Of course, he paid for the bottle of wine, and I'm certain he was banned from ever coming back. It reminded me of the *Seinfeld* episode where Kramer is banned from the fruit store.

It was not surprising to me that Evan was given the prestigious role of host and master of ceremonies of sorts at this Radcliffe Christmas Eve soiree. Outside in the tent, where dinner was to be served, everyone had a piece of paper beneath their plates. After dinner concluded, everyone would read from their piece of paper and act out whatever was written on the sheet. It could be a memory, a poem, a song, or a funny story.

Evan started the ceremonious reading of the papers by clinking his glass and yelling very loudly for everyone to shut up so we could commence the fun. The acoustics in the tent were extremely loud, and it was difficult to control the crowd with so many of us confined in this intimate space.

At some point it did quiet down, and we went around the room taking turns. It took about thirty minutes for my table to take its turn. Normally, everyone sits with people other than family members as part of the ritual. For some reason, Joe led me into the room and invited me to sit at his table. I was positioned across the table from Joe and between our friends Darren and Julie.

When Joe stood up for his turn, I noticed he seemed a little nervous. He had a card in his hand yet he wasn't asking a question. He started to make a toast. What was he doing? He began talking about how special this group of friends was, all of the ski trips they'd been on over the years, all the memories they'd created. Someone yelled out, "We're family!"

Then the conversation turned to ME! Joe said, "This is Jeanne's first year. A lot of you have met her. Darren introduced us."

Darren playfully said, "Don't hold that against me." I wasn't really sure where Joe was going with his little speech. In between, people were shouting out comments and talking amongst themselves. It was still very loud and I was confused.

Finally, Joe raised his glass and said, "I want to make this toast to Jeanne. To Jeanne." Everyone in the room raised their glass in unison. *What is he doing? This is really odd. Well, okay, I'll hold up my glass.* Joe moved his glass closer to my glass. Still confused, I completely missed the fact that a stunning diamond ring was perched on his pinky finger. He began to motion wildly with his pinky and remarked "HONEY!" to get my attention.

I finally noticed the ring. It was the most beautiful ring I had seen in my entire life. I remember thinking, is this really for me?

Everyone else in the room got it just about the same time I did. I think they were just as confused as I was until they saw the ring. I stood up from my chair and took the ring from his pinky while he held me tightly and whispered the words, "Will you marry me?"

He played it like a fairy tale. I was his princess. He put me on the pedestal. He did it in front of all his friends. Joe didn't disappoint. He made me believe that happily ever after was possible even at fifty-five years of age.

I could just see Shirley holding her cigarette and saying, "See, I told you so, didn't I?"

Chapter 28

A Vacation, a New Home, and a Wedding

Our wedding date was set for August 24, 2017. We had a Hussin family trip to Ireland planned for late July and that week in August was the only one available to accommodate most of Joe's very large family of six siblings along with my family and a circle of close friends.

Meanwhile, it was late May, and we were toying with the idea of purchasing a home together. Joe's Redmond home was comfortable and charming, yet it didn't deliver on closet space and didn't have enough room for overnight guests. Plus, having a home together would make it ours.

We considered the idea of adding onto Joe's home. We were also open to looking for a home we could purchase together. Without the help of a real estate agent, we started looking at open houses on the weekends. We were disappointed at some of the homes on the market. They often required more work than we cared to put into them, and we saw one too many kitchens that looked as if they'd been painted by a twelve-year-old. It wasn't looking good for us.

The Seattle housing market was booming. Houses would go on the market and often sell in one day with all-cash buyers winning out among the bidding wars. We agreed that we would only purchase a home if it ticked off all the boxes.

About a week before our family trip to Ireland, we decided to look at a house up the street from Darren and Julie. Located in a beautiful planned community with numerous parks, views of the Cascade Mountains, and easy access to the highways, we found ourselves inside a gorgeous relatively new John Buchan home.

The home featured a massive kitchen with a huge island, as well as ornate crown molding, etched glass, and a divine master bath with a soaking tub that called my name! We decided we would make an offer, knowing that it would most likely be declined.

I said to Joe, "How are we going to make this happen with our wedding practically a month away?"

As he often did, he calmly brushed aside my concerns and said, "We can do it. It won't be a problem." Joe had a way of making the tightest of demands seem not all that demanding.

Darren gave us the name of a real estate friend who would help us structure an offer right away. We submitted it on a Tuesday among all offers received. I kept thinking that it was a little crazy given that we worked full time, had a trip to Ireland planned in two weeks, and a big wedding coming in August. How in the hell could we move in that time period and retain our sanity? All the while, Joe kept telling me not to worry.

About two days after putting in our offer, our agent called me while I was working at my office. Rebecca was a stunning beauty who had been in the real estate business for over a decade. I answered the phone and she said, "Hi, Jeanne, it's Rebecca." I braced myself for the answer that must be a firm no. She began, "You know the house had multiple offers. One of the offers was all-cash and $15,000 higher than your offer." *I know where this is going*, I thought to myself.

Her next words almost sent me to my knees. "Jeanne, they accepted YOUR OFFER." I screamed in joy, shock, disbelief, excitement, and terror, knowing what was ahead of us with the wedding coming up.

"I can't believe it!" I shouted. "I just can't believe it. Oh my God, wait until I tell Joe. Well, I'll tell you it's a good thing I can't get pregnant!" A trip, a new home, and a wedding! That sounded like a box-office-hit comedy movie.

Prior to their acceptance of our offer, I had written a letter to the seller in the hopes that it would stir some emotions and make the seller more agreeable to our offer. I knew the owners had raised children in this home, and I understood the emotions of leaving a place with so many memories. Rebecca told me the owners were moved by my letter and had decided to take our offer.

7-11-17

Good afternoon,

My name is Jeanne and my soon-to-be husband's name is Joe Hussin. When I saw your chalkboard sign that read you loved living in your home, it melted my heart.

You see, I just sold my home in Simi Valley, California, where I raised my son as a single mom. It was a neighborhood very similar to yours, complete with a greenbelt.

As a single mom, my home was my solace and comfort. I felt intense joy that my son, Jason, had a beautiful place to rest his head every night and a breathtaking neighborhood where he could run, build forts, skateboard down the hill while I held my breath, sleep in a tent outside, collect and release lizards, hide homework that was due, and pretend he was a spy. So when I placed it for sale, it was very hard to say goodbye, and I would imagine that you have similar feelings about your home.

I moved to Washington last April because I fell in love with Joe. Joe is the kind of guy who always smiles. Everyone who meets Joe likes him, and I was no exception. He's an IT director and is a "Mr. Fix-It" type who appreciates fine craftsmanship. I'm a vice president of marketing and I love all things creative. (By the way, Joe doesn't trust me with sharp tools, so I let him do all the handiwork.)

He and I both love your home. The way in which you have cared for it says a lot about how special it was to you and your family. I know you created a lot of wonderful memories with your children and it shows.

Joe and I are getting married in August, and we're so excited about the thought of beginning our new life together in your exceptional home. This would be the best wedding present we could ever dream of or expect to find.

Thank you for your consideration. I wish you many happy memories ahead.

Kindest regards,

Jeanne (soon to be Mrs. Hussin, and I can't wait)

I waited the entire day before telling Joe. I wanted to see his expression when I told him we were about to be new home-owners. I could hardly wait to get home to him. I left work promptly at 5 p.m. and drove to our Redmond home. It was a beautiful summer day and the sun was shining brightly. The sun stays up well past 9 p.m. at that time of year, one of the things I love most about living here.

When I arrived home, the dogs happily greeted me. Joe was nowhere to be found. He was already working mornings and evenings to get the Redmond home ready for sale in the "unlikely event" we would move.

Joe likes to fix things, and he likes them to be perfect. Whether it was building me a she-shed, doing a complete room remodel, or hanging a picture on a wall, he worked like a master craftsman. I marveled at his massive hands. He had the dexterity of a surgeon, steady, strong, and stable. There is nothing sexier than a man who can build or fix things. I loved watching him work.

I found him out back on a ladder, doing some painting touch-ups on the house. I teased him, "What would be the best wedding present ever?"

He looked at me blankly and said, "What?" as if not really hearing me.

I repeated the question, "What would be the best wedding present ever?"

He replied with a question, "If we got the house?"

I nodded enthusiastically. "YES, they accepted our offer, Joe. They accepted it!"

"Stop messing with me!" he said.

I repeated the news and told him I was serious.

Startled and shocked by the news, he started shaking and almost fell off the ladder!

"You're serious, right? You're not joking," he exclaimed.

I finally convinced him we were going to move. Without missing a beat, he said, "Well, I've got a ton of work I gotta do," and picked up his paint brush.

Chapter 29

Ready. Set. Move.

I t was set. We'd move exactly five days before our wedding date. Are you SERIOUS?

Joe was the calm before the storm. We e-signed papers at midnight while in Ireland at the beautifully upgraded Kilkea Castle Estate and Golf Resort. The castle was located just one hour from Dublin. Although it was constructed in the ninth century, the castle was a newly renovated feast for the eyes. Surrounded by gardens, this boutique hotel was an amazing setting for our Hussin family reunion.

There were eleven Hussin family members staying at the resort. The intimate castle rooms were not quite ready for opening, so we stayed at the self-catering lodge, where we had plenty of space, privacy, and joint family rooms to convene. We enjoyed golf, dinners together on the castle grounds, a tour of the castle rooms, and other off-site tourist activities. I loved the people of Ireland and the entire historic experience of our stay at the castle.

Soon it was time to return home and begin packing. It was early August and we had less than three weeks to move into our new home. Our move-in date was only one week before our wedding date. Joe finished making improvements on the

Redmond home and it went on the market. In three days, he received multiple offers, and the house was sold for almost double what Joe paid for it. The market was nuts. The buyer made an offer and waived all contingencies.

The week leading up to our wedding, Joe flew my son out to help with our move. Jason would also give me away during the ceremony. Still feeling anxious and slightly overwhelmed, it was wonderful to have my two favorite men together under one roof. There was so much to do and so little time.

It was hard to believe this was my second move in less than two years. It's funny how even positive changes can leave you feeling unhinged and disconcerted. The move, the wedding, the after party, what was I thinking? My best friend thought I was nuts. "I could never do it," she said. "I think you're crazy." I started to think she was right.

One day as I began to unpack and stock the kitchen, I realized the kitchen cabinets had not been cleaned as well as we were led to believe. The previous owners had a deep cleaning ordered before we moved in. However, they were not up to my standards.

I looked at Joe with exasperation and complained like a whiny spoiled brat, "Oh my God, I've got to clean all these cabinets before I put everything away." The thought of doing all that power cleaning was just too much for me.

Joe said, "Don't worry, I'll take care of it." He told me to leave it with him and get some rest. The next day after work, he had everything cleaned up and put away. I felt badly that it was all on him. He didn't care. He just wanted to please me and wanted it done.

When I walked through the house that night, Joe and Jason planned a little prank to lighten the load. Joe greeted me at the front door with my favorite martini at the time, a green appletini, in his hand. I happily grabbed it from him as he said, "Now, honey, I know you've had a rough week and we just don't want you to ..." Before he finished his statement, I heard loud music piping throughout the house. It was the song "Le Freak" by Chic and Nile Rodgers. Written by American R&B band Chic, it was ranked the number 3 song by Billboard Magazine for 1979, the year I graduated from high school.

Joe and Jason had worked together to set up all the speakers throughout the house (there are built-in speakers in every room), connect music through Spotify, and queue up the song to just the right moment.

As the music played, they led me upstairs and we visited every room throughout the house, hearing the musical reminder that implied I freak out all too easily.

I had to laugh.

We laughed, we danced, we sang, and we connected as a family while making the rounds to the rooms that would become our new haven. The song became my theme song. And it certainly wasn't the last time I would freak out.

Chapter 30

The Big Day

After going round and round about what type of wedding we would have, we decided on Ray's Boathouse for the venue. We went from having an intimate seven-person wedding to a "$4,000 ice sculpture" or at least that's what Joe jokingly called it. While not exactly a star-studded locale, Ray's Boathouse had everything we wanted in a venue.

Located on the waterfront with a sweeping view of Puget Sound and the Olympic Mountains, it enabled us to get married right on the water with over fifty guests in attendance. This iconic fan-favorite restaurant was originally opened in 1945 by Ray Lichtenberger as a coffee house. In 1952, it became known as "RAY'S" and operated largely as a casual fish-and-chips café and boat rental. Then in 1973, it was purchased by new owners and refurbished as a nationally respected seafood restaurant.

In 1987, at the height of its popularity, Ray's Boathouse burned to the pier. A new boathouse emerged in April of 1988 only to suffer another fire nearly ten years to the date after its first fire. It later reopened in July of 1997.

The property featured the well-known restaurant along with the Northwest Room, which was steps away from the restaurant and accommodated groups of up to 225. We married on the adjacent outside dock at 6:00 in the evening on August 24, 2017. Cocktails were served to the right of the dock under a beautiful canopy featuring table tops and flowers.

While the weather in Seattle can be unpredictable, the sun made a fabulous appearance for our evening wedding with temps reaching into the comfortable seventies. It was my dream wedding and Joe was my dream man. After we exchanged vows and the minister announced, "You may kiss the bride," Joe took me in his arms and swung me into a surprise dip that gave the ceremony a little more personality!

I felt like a real-life Cinderella. I could not believe that at fifty-six years of age I felt more alive, more beautiful, and more loved than I could have possibly imagined.

My son, twenty-two at the time, walked me down the aisle and gave me away—all too happily, I might add. During our reception, he toasted us with a speech that would melt anyone's heart. A gifted writer with the ability to spit out eloquent words in the time it takes to say good morning, Jason had put together his speech the evening before our wedding.

"Three years ago when my mom came home from a business trip with a big grin on her face and told me she had met someone in Seattle, I was reluctant. The last thing I'd want for my mother is someone to hurt her. I just hoped that whoever she found was as compassionate, intelligent, and kind-hearted as her. Unfortunately, she found Joe.

"All jokes aside, I had no idea what to expect. I just knew that, above all, I wanted her to be happy.

"I wanted her to have a fruitful relationship with someone who could provide the support that she needed. Someone who could be there for her in times of struggle and doubt, and I'm pleased to say that she found the right man. A son couldn't ask for a better candidate to have his mother's heart.

"Fast-forward a little over a year, my mom decided to uproot her entire life of over thirty years and move to Washington. This move took an immense amount of strength and fortitude. This is the moment where I knew what they have must be special. She sold her house, left her friends in the rear view, and put it all on the line for the man she so dearly cherished. And now we're here.

"With this all being said, Joe, as of tonight, I officially gave her away. She's your problem now. If she's ever in a situation of need, it's up to you, no matter how difficult the issue may be. I've enforced a strict no-refund policy. So, Mom, if you need me for anything, I'm going to have to forward you to Joe. I can no longer assist.

"As a son, I haven't always been the best to my mother. Growing up we had a rocky relationship with one another. She always said when I was older I would appreciate the sacrifices she made for me. I would appreciate the groundings and the times of hardship. I never believed her. However, standing here today as a grown man, I can say I'm so thankful for how she raised me. All the vacations, gifts, and good times truly pale in comparison to how overwhelmed with joy I feel right now. The definition of joy is: a feeling of great pleasure and happiness. I think that just about hits the nail on the head for how we all feel.

"I wish nothing but the best for Joe and my mother. You two are some of the most hardworking people I've ever met. May you have a bright future, a happy retirement, and long lives."

I will never forget our wedding: the friends, the sun, the vows, my son, and the man who keeps me on that pedestal.

Coming Full Circle

S o here I am happily married, in my beautiful home, with an assisted living facility just ten minutes from my house. It's another Godwink moment, a sign, a duty, a cause, and an easy way for me to start giving back again.

The director is a charming woman about my age with a smile that never fades. She is all too happy to have me volunteer, and we've agreed I'll visit Saturday mornings.

After doing my usual "working of the room," as my showbiz mother would say, I find myself captivated by Faye. Faye is in her late eighties and when you talk to her you wonder if she's a resident by mistake.

She'll tell me she doesn't belong here. She's not like the others, and she feels as if she's lost all her independence. It makes me sad. Yet, I know the stories of these residents are never exactly as they appear to be.

Faye is sharply dressed and has stunning white hair combed back to reveal her gorgeous creamy complexion. She's an interior decorator, a painter, and a creator. She wears full makeup, blush, eyeshadow, and a soft, warm shade of light-pink lipstick that complements her white mane. She wears pearls and neat silver hoop earrings. I decide I want to look like her when I get to be her age.

In December, it's Faye who personally decorates most of the Christmas trees on display. The director suggested that

Faye bring all of her decorations with her when she moved into the home. She knew that it would give Faye a "job" and would help ease her transition.

Having a passion for anything that shines and is on display, I'm blown away by Faye's themed trees. There's the all-white tree adorned with a Polar Bear Express theme. Then there's a kiddie tree with storybook bears she created for her grandchildren. She even handmade beautiful doll ornaments with porcelain faces. Her attention to detail is incredible.

She is losing her memory more slowly than most, and she knows it. She plays nursemaid and mother to the ones who don't understand. We connect right away, and she loves my company.

Soon I meet Jacob. A tall, trim, gray-haired gentleman, he grew up in a Jewish family in the city of Tampa. He is a proud Vietnam veteran and a retired Boeing instructor who taught pilots how to run the instruments in the new planes. His wife, Connie, is a gentile. She agreed to convert and was accepted by the family with grace and love.

She was a nurse and he met her at a party for a group of military doctors. It appeared to be love at first sight. Jacob asks me quite frequently, "Have you seen Connie?" Always willing to placate, I tell him that I haven't yet and I know she will visit soon.

I learn bits and pieces from these beautiful souls by asking questions. I know which questions to ask and which ones to avoid. When I ask Jacob to tell me about his parents, I discover his father worked for Sears and Roebuck as a buyer and later became the owner of his own clothing shop. He wanted Jacob to take over the business.

With tears in his eyes, Jacob says, "I wanted nothing to

do with that business. I hated it, detested it. I didn't really appreciate my dad until much later in life and it was too late."

With a lump in my throat, I tell him, "Jacob, he is proud of you. He knows how much you loved him. I know that." It seems to settle him down a bit.

A lot of the residents relive these stories, riddled with guilt and regret. I feel their personal pain and say anything I can to alleviate misplaced guilt or shame so they can feel a sense of comfort, if only in that moment of time.

These stories become pieces of a puzzle I work to fit together. One day, Jacob walks around holding a wooden hanger. He grips it tightly as if it has some type of meaning. Upon closer inspection, I see an engraved name, "Terrytown Clothier." Aha, another puzzle piece.

"Jacob, that must be a hanger from your father's clothing store, right?" I say.

He brings the hanger up to eye level and spots the logo. "Why, yes," he remarks with emphatic surprise. "I found this in my room, and I wondered where it came from. Isn't that something?"

Jacob fails to remember that he brought the hanger with him when he moved into the home, a symbol of the father he respected and adored. His surprise and delight at having found it out of nowhere warms my heart. He tears up again, thinking about his dad. "I wish my dad knew how much I respected him." One-two-three, one-two-three, the dance repeats and I reassure him that he knew.

Then there's Vietnam. Jacob was in the army and served proudly during a conflict that wasn't popular. He taught air force pilots in Washington, DC, before being deployed. He mentions he saw a lot of guys die. He begins to weep and mutters, "That bullet wasn't meant for me."

Could this be survivor's guilt? It makes me sad knowing that, on top of suffering from dementia, he has to remember this. Why can't this memory be the one he forgets?

"Jacob," I say softly, "it wasn't meant for you. You were meant to help others and there's a reason you survived."

"I guess," he whispers softly, not fully accepting my answer.

I wonder whether these types of stressors in our lives, events that leave us with PTSD, tend to increase our risks of dementia. I read that older veterans who suffer PTSD are almost twice as likely to develop Alzheimer's disease and other age-related dementias as veterans without PTSD. There is other evidence that chronic stress may damage the hippocampus, which is the area of the brain that is critical for memory and learning.

It seems so unfair. It's like finally breaking free from a bad experience in life or being a victim and then getting hit by a car. How much should a person have to bear? I'm reminded that life is indeed unfair, so we must find a way to seek out the joy and find the small acts of kindness that give meaning to our lives whenever we can.

Chapter 31

A Book within a Book

It's hard and humbling to visit these beautiful souls who repeat the same lyrics of confusion.

"How can I get out of here?"

"Where is my wife?"

"I have nothing left."

"I don't understand why I'm here."

I hold their hands for a few moments, offering placating explanations that work for a few minutes. Then the lyrics and confusion repeat again.

"When can I go home?"

"I don't belong here."

"Have you seen my daughter?"

It must be frightening to be so confused and disoriented.

I had formed such a special connection with Faye that I decided to reach out to one of her daughters. It's nice to fill in all the pieces, and I've found that family members appreciate it when you visit and give them updates as I did when I lived in California.

I connected with her daughter Anitra on Facebook. Through my conversations with Faye, I knew that Anitra had lost her husband, her daughter, and her father all within a span of two years. Unconscionable. Unfair. Unbelievable.

I found out that she wrote a beautiful book called *Embracing Life from Death* detailing her journey through grief and healing. Her courage amazed me. I was so riveted by her story that I read it in one sitting. I can't think of another time I've read a book in one day. I usually fall asleep.

Even more amazing were the many parallels we shared in life. Like her, I fell madly in love with my husband later in life. Her romance played out like mine. She felt like a prom queen when she met her husband and felt sexier and more beautiful than she had her entire life. I felt the same way when I met my Joe.

Anitra and I also share the same birthday month and a love of art. A gifted artist, she began painting later in life and hasn't stopped. I believe it is self-soothing and helps her process her grief. I see in her what I've learned through my own experiences with grief: you don't get over losing your loved ones, you learn to live with it and help others.

Her book details ways to navigate the health care system, especially in instances when it seems overly complex. She's an inspiration to those who suffer enormous and tragic loss. Her husband and her grown daughter were both victims of cancer—her husband ravaged by brain cancer and her daughter by skin cancer. I wonder how in the world you go on after that? And now her mother was in the final stages of dementia. Really? Who gets that card handed to them?

Through reading her book, I learned more about her mom and their sometimes rocky relationship. I learned that Faye was legally separated from her husband, a fact that never came up during our conversations. I thought she was head over heels in love with him and that they danced together in their living room all the time. Perhaps it was the dementia and she only remembered the good parts about their relationship.

Reaching out to Anitra allowed me to connect to another soul who lives their life with meaning, with intent, with hope and purpose. Her story gave me another reason to see old people.

Being There

Be an Angel to someone else whenever you can, as a way of thanking God for the help your Angel has given you.

—Eileen Elias Freeman

K ris is ninety-seven. She's a living doll. Faye likes to engage with her. Kris was a nurse and her husband a pilot. She has three sons, one who drowned at age two. Faye knows of Kris's loss and says, "You never get over it." When I visit Kris, she tries to get out of her wheelchair. Unable to stand or walk, she asks me the same thing, "How do I get out of here?"

Did losing her child facilitate the loss of her memory? Of course, there's no way to know for sure. I hold her hand and tell her that it's time to eat soon and this is a nice place for her to be. I repeat this several times during our visit. One-two-three, one-two-three, the dance repeats. What else can I say or do?

And then there's John Krane. He's a quiet charmer with a bit of devilish spunk. John was a high school chemistry teacher who has nobility in his background. He tells me his family were dukes and had a castle in Sweden. His students affectionately called him Count K.

One day, I ask John if I can escort him into the "theater" where the residents gather to watch movies, listen to entertainment, or attend a church service. He tells me he will race me. He strikes a runner's pose and begins to "run" in a way that makes me think of Tim Conway's The Oldest Man character on *The Carol Burnett Show*.

That makes me laugh. Did John's playfulness extend into his teaching and into his personal life?

Sometimes I meet the families of these beautiful residents. I see the same man who attends to his wife almost every visit. She is stretched out in a reclining wheelchair and moans incoherently. She may speak an occasional word or two; even then it's only gibberish.

I talk to this man one day and ask about his wife. He tells me she's been here for about a year, and he comes to see her every day. They have two children and they used to travel often. I ask him how he's doing health wise. He pauses and then confesses he has Parkinson's disease. "I hope it's a slow progression," I say.

It's moments like these that I wonder if my visits are just as important to these families as they are to the residents. Maybe even more important. I make it a point to say hello and ask him how he's doing each time I visit.

A while back, I sat with a woman who was losing her mother. We sat side by side as she sobbed about her mother's deterioration. "She just changed overnight. It went so quickly, like flipping a switch. I can't believe it," she cried. I held her hand and told her I understood.

The fact is, from what I see, once this deterioration begins, it doesn't take long before it's over. I like to believe that at that point they regress to a more pleasant time. I saw that with my grandmother as she was dying. She kept thinking her children were young.

I pray that angels attend to these sweet souls when we can't be there with them. I have always feared death, even when I read about life-after-death stories. Although I'm a Christian by faith, I still have my doubts. I think of Matthew 17:20 when Jesus says that with the faith of a mustard seed we can move mountains. With faith, nothing is impossible. With a tiny bit of faith, there is a way.

That gives me hope, it gives me courage, and it gives me the energy to encourage kindness and compassion. We can't control most things that happen in our lives. We can only control our reactions. We can choose to be kind creatures. We all need to feel that we matter, no matter what age, no matter who we are.

If we are kind, nothing will be impossible for us.

Chapter 32

Showing Up

In my twenties, my cousin Paul nicknamed me Monitor Lady—not a flattering nickname. He called me Monitor Lady because I was hell-bent on controlling everything and everyone around me.

I'm not sure if it's because I was born that way or because I was the middle child of an alcoholic. Either way, I wanted to control everything I could for fear an unimaginable catastrophe would somehow ruin my life.

I worried not only about what people thought of me, but also what they thought of my friends, my family, and my first husband. I felt a strange responsibility for others' actions that had nothing to do with me. It was so all-consuming that I'm certain I was a very uptight person to be around.

It wasn't until my later years that I let go of trying to control everything. When I realized that most of the things I worried about never happened, experience weighed in and told me to just let it go! The only thing I could control was me. I could even control my compunction to control others. What a concept!

Today this letting go serves me in many ways. In a world that appears to be going haywire, it puts me in the driver's seat to focus on the things I can do that will help others. In turn, it makes me feel that I have the control to shape my destiny.

This life lesson has served me well. It spurred me to take small action steps when I needed to change my circumstance. It was not intended to solve all my problems or the problems on this planet. Rather, it made me feel that if I made conscious choices, I could eventually land in a better place.

Giving back in small ways paid big personal dividends. Holding the hand of a lonely soul, helping a grief-stricken friend, donating to a food bank, or giving a stranger a compliment. (Try it sometime. You may receive an incredible reaction.) It showed me I had the power to do something meaningful, to create change in this world, even if on a very small scale.

It starts with a simple action: show up. I think we can all feel paralyzed and that stops us from doing just about everything. When you show up in the present moment and let kindness lead, you find the energy to fulfill your intention.

I'll give you an example. You decide to exercise for thirty minutes in the morning. When the morning comes, it's the last thing you want to do. Somehow you find your way to the elliptical machine in the garage. You're dead tired, so you tell yourself you'll do ten minutes and that's it. *That will have to be good enough*, you say to yourself.

Before you know it, forty-five minutes have passed and you feel great. You sweated, you worked out to the music, and you did far more than a ten-minute workout. And why? Because you showed up.

Giving back works the same way. If you sit down to write that heartfelt "I care" card, if you get in your car to go pick up the gift for the sick neighbor, if you visit a GoFundMe page to make a donation, you've taken the most difficult step of all. You showed up.

While I still have a bit of "Monitor Lady" in my DNA—just ask my husband—I'm a lot less inclined to control every person and event in my life. I'm learning the most important step of all is showing up. The rest takes care of itself.

A Story within a Story

When I walk into a memory care facility, I never know what to expect. Sometimes the residents are confused. Oftentimes, many are confused at the same time.

Other times, there are a number of highly lucid residents open to my conversation, laughing at my jokes, and telling me stories that are rich in history and character. Some even contain a bit of saucy naughtiness.

Today I went in to see my favorite, Faye. She is starting to succumb to the dementia that is slowly taking away everything that I love about her, so I want to visit with her for as long as I can.

I know she will have good days and bad days in the months ahead, so I'm pleasantly surprised she recognizes me. "Hello. Where have you been?" she says in her customary style.

We strike up our usual conversation, and she wants to know all about what's new with me. We talk mostly about things I know will make her smile. Her husband's dancing, her time with her son at Christmas, visiting the Space Needle, and all things creative.

At some point I turn to another resident and Faye is gone. I can't spot her anywhere. I notice a man with a small black mutt and start to ask him about his dog. I learn that his dog, Nick, is his salvation. He's an attractive man in his sixties with a white goatee, pierced ears adorned with small diamonds, and a nice jacket with a cross pin.

He tells me he lost two dogs and then tragically lost a son.

I tell him I'm sorry for his loss. Then he explains how he found his new dog, Nick, online. "Ever lose a dog as an adult?" he asks, knowing that there is a big difference between experiencing a pet's death as an adult versus as a child. When you're a kid, you bounce back. When you're an adult, bouncing back isn't in the equation.

"No, I haven't."

I don't even want to think about the pain I will face when the time comes for my dogs.

A new resident I don't recognize shuffles toward us with her walker. She appears to be in her eighties and has white hair pulled back in a squared bun and a full set of dentures. "When I lived on the farm in the hills of West Virginia, we had collies," she says, bending over to pat Nick on the head.

"Collies are the best, and I had one that I loved," she announces with a grin. Her Southern drawl drips with sweetness and frothy charm.

This woman is about to tell me her life story.

Sure enough, she dives right in.

Her name is Brenda Jean, nicknamed "Brenda Boy" by her father. "I would wait until Daddy went to sleep and sneak that dog into my bed," she says. "Then in the morning, I would wake up before Momma got up to make sure I took the dog back outside."

She explains that her family said animals aren't meant to be inside. She tells me more about her upbringing and about how she met her husband, a World War II military veteran who went on to become a port engineer in Louisiana. They met at a dance club and married within nine days. "I don't want you to think I'm a slut," she quips. Now my ears really perk up, awaiting a salacious story.

She explains there were hundreds of women who frequented dance clubs at that time, looking for military men. "I wasn't one of them. Back then, you had to be examined for venereal diseases. I'm sure you know about that."

I don't. I just nod to encourage her to go on.

"*These* women would go to these clubs looking for men and this was a real concern because they carried diseases," she said emphatically. "It was only a blood test. Still, I didn't want to be tested," she said.

Later I did some cursory research online and read that USO clubs were organized to protect soldiers from negative influences, including "disreputable women." The men could meet the "right kind" of women through supervised dances with carefully screened young women and legions of chaperones. Perhaps this is what my Brenda Boy was referencing.

She tells me a cousin persuaded her to go the dance club that night, and the rest is history. She and her future husband went to a church nearby and spent all night talking. Nine days later, they got hitched.

Her husband was born in the United States to parents of German descent, so he spoke fluent German. When his parents spoke German in front of her, it really pissed her off. She points her finger at me as if to scold me. "One day, I'm in the middle of their living room, and they start speaking that German. I said to them, 'I don't give a damn about what you do. If you don't start speaking English to me, I'm out of here.'"

She started to walk out of the room and told her husband

that he could stay or go. Her mother-in-law jumped up and admonished her son to chase after his wife.

"Wow, Brenda, you didn't mince words. How was your relationship after that?"

Brenda smiles with a know-it-all smirk. "It was perfect. We were close after that. I nursed my husband's daddy when he was dying. He drank his-self to death. Drinking whiskey, that done there killed him."

Brenda is on my list of new friends to visit. And just when it appears that Brenda has all her faculties, she tells a visitor that she works at the memory care facility. I wonder what she thinks she does.

I learn that Brenda has four or five children. It's not atypical for my seniors to forget the number of children they have or whether they have any at all. One daughter is a pharmaceuticals patent attorney. Another, Regina, is mentally challenged and works at Safeway. "She's the sweetest one of all," she says with a smile and affirming nod.

My respect for Brenda immediately grows. She's one of those people who is tough on the outside and warm and fuzzy on the inside. Probably not one to show public affection, she'd be the first one you'd call on in a crisis. I sense she hasn't had an easy life.

In the end, our stories are the fabric of who we are and what we aspire to be. I can't wait to hear more of Brenda's stories.

Chapter 33

Senior Visits

To give somebody your time is the biggest gift you can give.

–Franka Potente

Most days I don't get up thinking, *I really want to visit seniors today. I can hardly wait to get there.* I have to push myself. Joe always tells me, "Jeanne, you should go. You always come back in a really good mood."

He's right of course. When I visit, I make a connection, experience a moment, and after, I feel gratitude, have a sense of purpose, and even feel hopeful. I'm making a difference in the world even by giving an hour of my time.

The gift of time is worth more than any gift in the world. You can't buy it. You can't fake it. You can't get enough of it.

Children often prefer spending one-on-one quality time with a parent over receiving a gift. One of the saddest songs I've heard is "Cat's in the Cradle" by Harry Chapin. It's about a little boy growing up and wishing to spend time with his dad. He wants to be just like his dad, but his dad isn't available. Ironically, when the little boy grows up, he becomes just like his dad. He doesn't have time for his aging father, who wishes to spend time with him.

I wish I'd had more time with my mom before she passed. So now, I spend my time with seniors not much older than me. Each of them has a story, a family, a life that mattered. Each one has something to give that is far greater than we might imagine. If only we'd listen.

A moment of comfort is the most I can give. I try to ask questions that will invite a spark of light.

"What was your favorite vacation?"

"What holiday did you like the most?"

"What's your favorite song lyric?"

"What was your favorite hobby?"

Sometimes I get surprising answers. Sometimes I come up empty. If I get an answer that sparks joy, I store it in my memory bank and replay the question the next time I visit. After all, it's unlikely they will remember our conversation.

Memories are everything. My mom would sit on the front steps of our house and think a lot. I imagine she revisited times spent playing music with my dad, working in Las Vegas with him, or being in the center of an adoring crowd of fans.

Good memories give us a safe place to visit when life deals us a blow. They are sacred. They are movie reels of our history that play out for our own personal enjoyment. They are a gift of time well spent.

Chapter 34

COVID-19

*Godwinks are the reassuring signposts along your path
letting you know you're going in the right direction.*

—Squire Rushnell, *Divine Alignment*

By April 2020, COVID-19 had become a reality in the US. The world changed and everything felt as if it was turned upside down. I was almost finished writing my memoir and the stories about my visits with seniors who suffer from dementia. Now that I could no longer visit my friends at the senior home because of the virus, I poured my creative energies into completing my book. While I wanted it to have a happy ending, I wasn't sure how my story should end.

Writing is like painting. I'm never done. I'm never satisfied. I see the fine details I can add to make it a little more perfect. *If I add this shading over here, there will be more depth. This sunrise should have more yellow.*

I felt that way about my book. What was I forgetting? What powerful message was I missing? Would people even read it?

Then something happened that took my breath away. You could say it was nothing short of a Godwink moment, those seemingly coincidental moments I first read about in *Divine Alignment* that are too aligned to be a fluke.

In early April, I posted a note on my neighborhood Facebook page. "Does anyone make masks? I'd like to buy a few." I got a response from a neighbor I didn't know, Norma. She wrote that she sews masks and would leave them for me in the morning on her front porch.

As promised, Norma sewed three masks for me—she even made one with Seahawk colors for Joe. I tried to pay her. She refused to accept. Humbled by her act of kindness, I picked up the masks from her doorstep and left her a nice bottle of wine and a handwritten thank you card.

We became Facebook friends and soon learned we have a lot in common. She's an artist and a poet, she loves dogs, and she even shares my appetite for Maker's Mark.

I'm going to love this girl, I thought. I couldn't wait to meet up with her and connect. With life up in the air at the beginning of the pandemic, I had no idea when that would be.

Mid-April, Norma wrote a poem about her father and posted it to her Facebook page. He was lying in the hospital, sick with COVID-19. I responded with heartfelt prayers and words of comfort. How devastating to have a loved one in that situation. It was my worst nightmare to die alone, to die without family. It frightened me to the core.

A few days later, Norma's husband posted to say that, sadly, Norma's father had passed. I read her father's name. *Oh my God.* I read it again. I screamed in disbelief. I realized that Norma's dad was Jacob, one of my favorite residents at the senior home I visit.

I ran to tell my husband the news. "You're not going to believe this coincidence," I told him, reminding him that Jacob was the Vietnam vet, the retired Boeing instructor whose father owned the clothing store, Terrytown Clothier.

I rushed to send Norma a private message about my relationship with her dad. I let her know there was a chapter in my book about him.

Norma, I'm so sorry to learn about your dad. I believe your dad is one of the seniors I visit at Firestone. I'm a volunteer there. On the weekends, I visit with seniors and hold their hands. He was my favorite. When you're ready, we should talk by phone.

Norma responded to my message right away. She confirmed her dad, Jacob, was the senior I visited. She wrote, "God works in mysterious ways, and we were meant to meet. Yes, my dad was taken from Covid-19. He is no longer suffering from dementia and no longer gasping for air. I'm relieved yet overcome with emotions beyond description."

She told me she believes in miracles. She had an overwhelming sense of happiness among the sadness and tears. I think it's because these divine moments make us believe there really is a God who seeks to connect us. There really is divine alignment when we look closely.

Later, we met again in person—at a distance—talking from her driveway.

She extended her arms out to me, her eyes full of tears. "I want to hug you so badly."

I wanted to hug her too. Yet, I'm so glad I could see her, speak with her, and comfort her. I was humbled and astounded.

Norma said, "Jeanne, I'm not really a religious person. I suppose I'm spiritual in a way. Yet, this makes me feel even more connected to something bigger. I truly believe my dad was a conduit to our meeting."

My question about finishing my book was answered for

me. I saw clearly how a kind act from a perfect stranger was not a coincidence. Norma and I both felt comforted knowing we had a common bond.

I knew this was *divine alignment*. I knew this was the purpose for my story. This is a story that needs to be told. Now more than ever.

Chapter 35

Kindness Is Hot

Seduce my mind and you can have my body,
find my soul and I'm yours forever.

−M.D. Waters, *Archetype*

Joe and I have known each other for six years now, and we've been married for three. Our passion is as strong as it was when we met, if not stronger. I marveled again at my good fortune, to have found love in this chapter of my life. My mother once told me that friendship can turn into passion very quickly when you like the other person. That happened to me with Joe.

I remember my mother telling me the story of the love affair she had with my dad. She wasn't immediately smitten nor convinced she should even date him. Yet before long, his uncommon character traits won her affections. He was persistent, affectionate, and undauntedly convinced my mother was the one.

Kindness is a BIG aphrodisiac. Joe has kindness oozing from his pores.

One of his married female friends once said to me, "We didn't want to like you."

"What do you mean?"

She explained, "Joe's a great guy. Most of us like him better than our own husbands. We're very protective of him. We never thought he would meet someone worthy enough to have him."

Thankfully, they did like me. If they hadn't, I don't know if I would be here writing this today. For those seeking love, the kind that lasts a lifetime, genuine kindness is easy to spot. Look for it in public places. How does a man talk to the parking lot attendant, the waitress, the nurse, the flight attendant, his friends, or the trash collector? That will tell you all you need to know.

My mom often told me that passion starts in the kitchen. At the time I didn't exactly understand what she meant. Now I know that how you're treated in other rooms of the house ultimately factors into whether you have sex or not. If you have a kind conversation beforehand, chances are, you'll get lucky.

My father was kind to everyone. Before he died, he was part of a local union band that worked the Ringling Bros. and Barnum & Bailey circus every year. This was way before the circus transitioned to using canned music.

My brothers and I were treated to front row tickets to see the show. When we arrived, my dad took us backstage to meet the acts. I remember feeling so important, even as a nine-year-old. There were a number of circus clowns that knew him quite well. They addressed him by name and scooped me up into a big hug.

I remember one man was a small person, and he hugged me like I was his own little girl. It delighted me no end. It felt like I was meeting a celebrity.

There was a clown named Dougy who was one of the "boss" clowns and the leader of the clown unit. He remembered us every year and made a point to chat with my mom and dad before the show.

After my father died, the last thing my mother wanted to do was return to the circus. Still, I begged her until she could no longer take it. She relented and took us to see the greatest show on earth.

Dougy made a point of coming over to my mother. "Shirley, I was so saddened to learn about Dick. He was beloved by so many of us. I can't imagine your loss."

My mother told me she'd greatly appreciated his act of kindness. He'd remembered my dad. He'd remembered our family. He'd taken the time to show how much he cared. I'll never forget that moment.

Kindness is never forgotten. Long after you're gone, people will remember you for how you made them feel.

I wish I had told my younger self to look for kindness. Instead, I sought drama and edginess. I would tell any young person to pick someone kind. You'll never fall out of love with kindness. Never.

Chapter 36

To Screams of Love

Family. A little bit of crazy, a little bit of loud, and a whole lot of love.

−Unknown

One night, Joe and I watched a movie starring Adam Sandler and Chris Rock called *The Week Of*. It's a comedy about two fathers from different worlds preparing for their children's wedding. Adam's character, Kenny Lustig, is the father of the bride, struggling to pay for his daughter's wedding and give her the gift of a lifetime. Of modest means, the best he can afford for a venue is a two-star Quality Inn.

Chris Rock plays Kirby Cordice, the father of the groom, who attempts multiple times to rescue Kenny from a wedding disaster and host the wedding at a ritzy locale. Despite all of Kenny's character flaws, he has a heart of gold and he offers the gift of time for his kids while Kirby, a successful surgeon, does not. In the end, the time and attention win out over all the money and glitz.

Even more amusing to me is the yelling match between Kenny and his wife, Debbie, played by Rachel Dratch. They hole up in their upstairs bedroom with the doors shut to protect the rest of the family from overhearing the argument. It's no use—the shouting is as deafening as a 747 coming in for a landing.

Growing up, my family yelled. Not just a little. They yelled a lot. It was all I knew, so I thought it was normal. My mother would yell even if we had visitors. She'd walk to the basement entrance, fling open the door, violently flick the lights, and scream down the basement steps in highly syncopated tones, "WILL YOUUUUUU TURNNN THAT DOWN? I'M NOT GOING TO ASK YOU AGAIN."

This was in response to my brother, who loved to blare "In-A-Gadda-Da-Vida" by Iron Butterfly from his stereo. He'd persist in turning the volume up despite my mother's antics.

I'm not sure what our visitors made of it. Even with all the shouting, I always felt loved. Like my father did, my mother put me on a pedestal. "Jeanne, you have it all. You are pretty. You are smart. You can do anything you set your mind to do," she said. I think it's why I always had such confidence in my life. I felt pretty. I felt smart. I felt empowered.

I guess my point is that we all have imperfections. We have character flaws. We have dysfunction in our families. We have failures. I admit that I inherited my mother's propensity for shouting, although I do very little of that today.

I find my mother's character flaws to be poetically comedic. Speaking of her parenting, she used to tell me, "There was a lot I did wrong, and there was a lot I did right. I really didn't enjoy the toddler years. I much preferred when you were more grown up."

I'm sure there was some yelling going on during those toddler years. It was that way with my son too. I remember shouting at Jason when he was only four because he refused to potty train. I watched him as he looked at me in fear and disbelief. If I could turn back the clock, I'd handle things differently.

I hope he won't remember those hard days. As with my mom and me, I hope he remembers the good. In hindsight, her shouting doesn't seem so bad. The confidence, encouragement, and time that my mother gave me is what sticks with me today.

I'll take a little bit of crazy and a lot of love any day of the week.

Epilogue

"Jeanne, you never know what's around the corner." My mother often said this to me when something upsetting happened, like a breakup or a job loss. It gave me hope that something wonderful was on the way.

It sounds like magical thinking, and yet ... wonderful things did happen for me throughout my lifetime. The biggest surprise of all was finding the greatest love of my life in midlife, finding THE man who puts me on the pedestal. Somehow I felt that Shirley was there for that one.

She was my biggest fan even when I wasn't qualified. I remember when I was about seventeen, and I tried out for a musical theater production. She played the piano accompaniment while I sang "What I Did for Love," a song from the musical *A Chorus Line* by Marvin Hamlisch. I was off-key and nervous. I failed miserably. I was so angry and resentful that I didn't have her pitch. I didn't have her musicality. I didn't have her talent.

Mom put her arms around me and pulled me close. "Honey, there will be other auditions. This will not be your last." I didn't believe her. With a delivery to rival Scarlett O'Hara, I said I would *never* audition again. Of course, I did, even if I didn't become the Broadway star I hoped to be.

What I know now, though I didn't realize it then, is that I inherited her passion, her confidence, and her compassion—gifts that inspired my creativity and my belief that I could make a difference in this world. I believe that is true for every person.

When I was a little girl, my mom sang and played a love song to me called "I Wish You Love" about the ending of a love that couldn't work. Despite the hurt, the singer wishes her departing lover only good things as the romance ends.

My mom would coo to me, "I wish yoooooooouuuuu LOVE." That song always reminded me that it's possible to forgive. It's possible to be kind. It's possible to love again. And I did just that.

Author's Note

All our dreams can come true, if we have the courage to pursue them.
      —Walt Disney

I have dreamed of writing a book for over twenty-five years. I saw writing as a means to becoming a comedienne and an actress—another dream of mine. I envisioned myself writing a bestseller that would land me on *Ellen* or *Oprah*. In the meantime, I'm deeply committed to philanthropic work, something I'm ardently passionate about, especially when it comes to helping seniors.

I started this book sometime around 2010 and then stopped writing. I continued to tell everyone I knew that I would write a book someday. The years passed and someday still seemed a long way off. Then in January of 2019, I decided to pick up where I left off.

When I looked back and read my unfinished manuscript, I thought, *Wow, some of this would resonate today.* I wondered why I had waited so long to finish my book. Then it hit me: I was waiting until I had more to say. In 2010, I wasn't dreaming of finding the greatest love of my life and moving to Seattle to get married for the second time.

Now I had a REAL story to tell! Always one to write out my dreams and goals, I've learned that sometimes dreams really do come true. They just may not happen overnight.

I found love. I found inspiration. I found a way to make a difference. And my story continues to unfold. I hope my story will inspire anyone who feels overwhelmed, insignificant, or alone to feel safe and encouraged. Hope is eternal.

If I can impart three things to take away from my story, they are:

1. It's never too late to do something you dream about.
2. Love is always possible when you open your heart.
3. The hardest part about giving back is showing up.

Moments & Memories

Jason and me at the circus

Jason and me

Me with Jason in costume

Jason and me at Disneyland

Jason and me at my wedding

Jason and Tasha

Jason and me at a Dodgers game

Standing with Jason at my wedding

Joe and me at a friend's house near Puget Sound

Joe with Tasha Bear (left) and Oscar (right)

Joe and me at the cabin

Joe and me, The Resort at Pelican Hill

Joe and me on our wedding day

We're getting married!

Joe and me on vacation

Joe and I steal a romantic moment on our wedding day

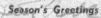

*Shirley and Dick in the Dunes playbill -
autographed by actress Bette Grable*

GABE — SHIRLEY — DICK

Shirley

Shirley and her band

Mom and Dad in Vegas at Christmas time

LAS VEGAS • DEC • 56

184

About the Author

Jeanne Corvese Hussin is a chief marketing officer for a financial services company based in Seattle. A compelling storyteller, she has over thirty years' experience in brand marketing and public speaking.

In 2008 Jeanne was an unemployed single mother who had given up on finding Mr. Right, so she decided it was time to give back. Visiting Recollections, a local assisted living facility for seniors with dementia, Jeanne took her first steps down a path of joy, fulfillment, and personal transformation.

Landing a full-time position as an executive for a Seattle-based company, Jeanne worked remotely and traveled to the Pacific Northwest on a monthly basis. It was there she met a handsome stranger who captivated her heart and changed her life. She packed up and moved to Seattle in 2016, where she married Joe one year later.

Today Jeanne resides in Washington with her husband and their two dachshund mixes, Tasha Bear and Oscar. She volunteers her time visiting with seniors who suffer from dementia and enjoys spending time with her son, Jason.

You can visit Jeanne at www.kindconversations.com. She loves to hear from her readers.

CPSIA information can be obtained
at www.ICGtesting.com
Printed in the USA
LVHW090058270621
691133LV00030B/447/J